SIGNS
OF OUR
TIMES

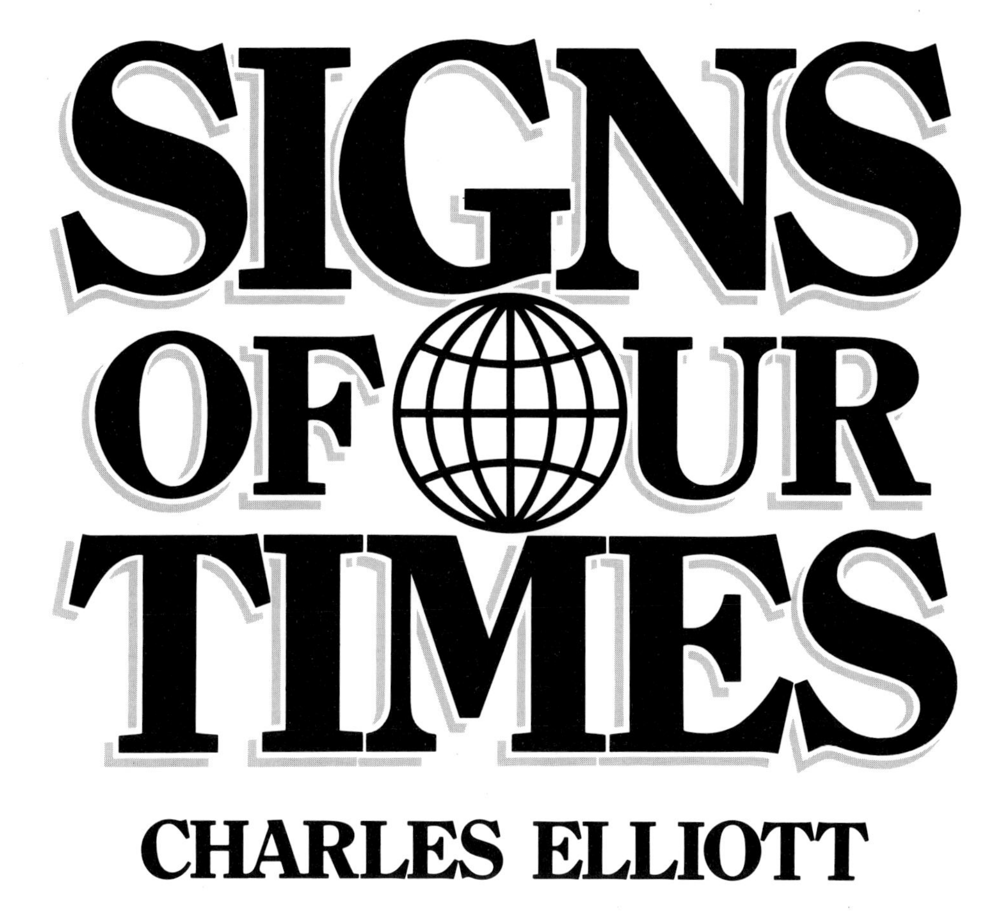


CHARLES ELLIOTT

MARSHALL PICKERING

Marshall Morgan and Scott
Marshall Pickering
3 Beggarwood Lane, Basingstoke, Hants RG23 7LP, UK


First published in 1988 by
Marshall Morgan and Scott Publications Ltd.;
part of the Marshall Pickering Holdings Group,
a subsidiary of the Zondervan Corporation.



**British Library Cataloguing in Publication Data**

Elliott, Charles, *1939–*
Signs of our times.
1. Socioeconomic problems. Role of Christian church
I. Title
261.8

ISBN 0–551–01664–7

Designed by Tony Cantale Graphics

Text set in Melior by Watermark, Hampermill Cottage,
Watford WD1 4PL

Printed and bound in Great Britain by
Butler & Tanner Ltd, Frome and London

# Contents

## PICTURE ACKNOWLEDGMENTS

Afrapix, page 11
Art Directors, 171, 172, 181, 183
The Bettmann Archive, 34
Christian CND, 17
Earthscan, 63
Format Photographers, 33 bottom, 36, 83, 98, 142, 142/3, 169
Barbara Heller/Fay Godwin, 107, 109
International Defence & Aid Fund, 197
Chris Kapollea, 180
Mary Evans Picture Library, 71
Network, 31
Panos Pictures, 26, 28/9, 33 top, 79, 147
Photo Co-op, 25
Rex Features/Sipa Press, 123, 127, 130, 131, 135, 136/7, 136, 137, 157, 165, 185
Seaphot Ltd: Planet Earth Pictures, 62, 67, 68
ZEFA Picture Library (UK) Ltd, 68, 89, 101, 102

Cartoons on pages 49, 75, 95 & 145 are by Len Munnik

# Acknowledgments

I am pleased to acknowledge the help of the many people who contributed to this book. Jonathan Elliott did much of the original research and thereby saved me many hours of trailing round specialist libraries. From nearly all of those he—and in some cases, subsequently I—visited, we received much good natured and well informed help. It is a privilege to record our debt to the librarians and researchers who gave it so cheerfully.

Debbie Thorpe at Marshall Pickering was a never failing source of encouragement as a patient midwife. When the nature of the book shifted suddenly and decisively towards the end of labour, she adjured the author to heartier heaves and expressed confidence that the birth would have a happy ending. I hope she is not disappointed.

Kate Talbot put the manuscript on disc and thus accelerated the editing and polishing. Her speed, efficiency and energy are becoming legendary among those who know her and I am delighted to have furnished some of the raw material for that legend.

To my colleagues in the Institute of Contemporary Spirituality, I perhaps owe the biggest debt of all. It was they who made me see the need for a book such as this and helped me to see how the various components could be integrated. Naming individuals is always as invidious as refusing to name them is ungenerous, so I say a warm thank you to Madeleine Prendergast, Gerry Hughes SJ, Graham Chadwick, Linda Mary Evans, and very specially, to Hilary, my wife. I accordingly dedicate this book to them and our common work.

CHARLES ELLIOTT

# INTRODUCTION

I believe God acts in history. Our history.

I do not believe he acts only or even mainly through the Church. He's too big a God for that.

He acts in the great events of our day. In the crises, the opportunities, the 'new things' that are constantly splashed across our headlines.

We do not see him there because we have never been encouraged to look there, even though we may have read our Old Testaments and tried to see history through the eyes of Isaiah and Jeremiah and Amos.

But what sort of God acts in our contemporary history—in Ethiopia and Mozambique; in Congress and Parliament; in factory and trade union? If he's God, why doesn't he deliver us from the nightmare of starving people, of arms expenditures seemingly still out of control, of homelessness and poverty in our own inner cities, of alienation and anomie that can only express themselves in violence?

But to say that, is to ask for a God who robs us of responsibility, a God of magic rather than of mystery and miracle, a God who will wave his wand and relieve us of the need to grow up. Sometimes that is the kind of God we crave, one who will solve all our problems for us. A Sugar Daddy God.

We don't have a Sugar Daddy God. The cross showed that.

But the resurrection revealed that we have a God who will not be beaten, a God who ushers in something so new, something so beyond our expectation, that we fail to recognise it, even when it's all around us.

It's that that fascinates me—and it's that that this book is all about.

I think we are at a turning point in our history. Some people call it the new age. Others say it is the end of the dominance of the scientific method, or the birth of the new consciousness, or the alternative consciousness. A phrase I shall use a lot in this book and which I will explain shortly is *the kairos*. The language doesn't matter much. The facts behind the language do.

And what are those facts? Simply that we cannot go on as we are. If we do, we shall blow each other to pieces. Or pollute each other to extinction. Or leave two thirds of us to die in poverty and disease, while too many of us live in intolerable conditions, physically and emotionally. We are coming to the end of the road of this kind of living.

I believe God is active in the events of our times to make us see that and lead us into new, more healthful, kinds of living. He chooses many ways of making us see, and different ways for different sorts of people. So we find some people saying that we have been seduced by the blandishments of science into thinking that we can live by the 'is' and forget the 'ought', that science has offered us the dead end of the positive and is now, a little belatedly, beginning to wonder about the normative. Others say that our technological sophistication has run ahead of our wisdom, so that we have become possessed of the means while remaining morally incapable of specifying the ends.

Those who speak or hear the more traditional language of the Christian faith say that our problems arise from the fact that we have tended to forget that humankind is the subject of the Fall; that as a race we are constantly in need of release from the self-worship that so persistently and voraciously consumes us. They say that now, as the crises of our own making wind their menacing tentacles around our future, we are—perhaps too late—awaking to our fate.

I suspect that all these points of angst-ridden view boil down to much the same perception: that we have a choice to make. Either we can go on as we are and face the consequences, certain of only one thing: that the consequences will be unpleasant; or we can undergo a change in our inner essence so fundamental that the future becomes liveable again.

That should not surprise us. For we know that there is something deep within the whole of creation that insists that the price of survival is change. But there lies the rub. How can we change—especially when the scale, the moral order, of change that is demanded of us, is so far beyond our ken? It is at that point that many people give up. To them the order of change required is so other, so beyond the possibility of their imagining, that they despair. 'It simply cannot happen,' they say, and, presumably, prepare for the worst.

I have a great sympathy for them. At times, I admit, I share their despair. It is at those times that I am driven back to the faith and to

In South Africa, the Christian faith comes up against one of the clearest signs of a broken world: the oppression of humans by humans.

the biblical record on which it is based. There I find a God who re-creates and redeems his people, not as a tyrant who robs them of their free will, but as a lover who gives them the possibility of growing into their fullest potential. And the instrument he seems to choose is the kairos.

The kairos is the moment of creative opportunity; the moment in history—political, social, personal history—that demands a courageous, trusting response. It may seem, as it seemed to Isaiah and Jeremiah, a moment of crisis, when the future is unclear or threatening. Or it may, as in the most striking of all examples of kairos, be a moment of great liberation. 'Now,' said Jesus, 'is the acceptable time.' With Jesus, the kairos of God's decisive act in history had arrived, and men and women had to decide how they would respond to that act.

These two features are the marks of the kairos: the initiative of God and the response of the people. But God does not hit us over the head with the kairos. It has to be discerned, to be detected among the flux and confusion of everyday events.

And that is what this book is really about. It is first and foremost a guide to where I think there is reason to think that God is showing us the possibilities of a creative response; where he is calling us to see things in a new light, from a new perspective, so that we can change our ways.

For example, the ecological crisis that threatens us on so many fronts is—or can be seen by the eye of faith as being—a call to change our habit of exploiting the natural environment. The rising sense of alienation from all social structures that is expressed in delinquency, vandalism and despair can be seen as a call to change the way we allow power to be concentrated in fewer and fewer hands, leaving the rest of us unable to take responsibility for our own lives. The fact that there are more desperately poor people than ever in a world that has never known such affluence is a call, surely, to look again at the way we organise our relationships with the poor of the earth.

'But,' says Mr Goodheart,'what am I going to *do* about it? I don't want to read yet more books that are going to leave me feeling overwhelmed by the size of the problem and the inadequacy of my resources.'

Quite.

So what we need is a way of approaching the 'kairos areas' that allows us to discern the purposes of God through the curtain of events; and enables us to respond in a way that will further, rather than impede, those purposes—a guide to the spirituality of action.

The diagram below suggests one such way. (It is not, of course, the only way; but it is the way that I shall be exploring more systematically in this book.)

At the centre lies what I have called 'Reflection on the love of

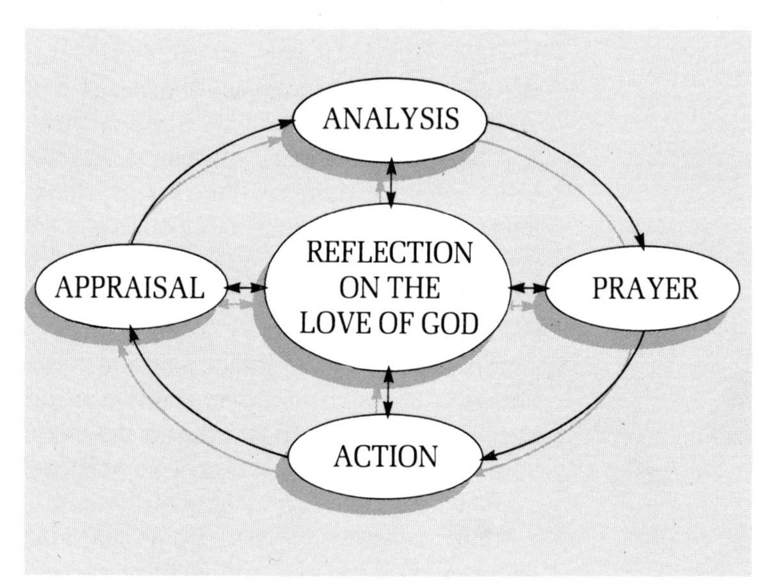

God'. There is no one method that will put us in touch with the reality of that love, not least because we are made differently and what 'works' for one person will not necessarily work for another. In the chapters that follow I shall be suggesting a number of approaches that I find helpful. Most of them are based, in one way or another, on the Bible, for it is there that we find the most comprehensive recollections of what God has done for his people. As we shall discover, there are a variety of ways of reading the Bible and we may well find that we need to explore them all to allow the full grandeur of the love of God so to possess us that even the scariest implications of the kairos do not frighten us.

I want to emphasise that. I have written this book out of the conviction that we are being called out of the ways of the past into a new way of living, a new way of expressing our love to each other and to God. None of us finds change easy or agreeable—especially when it is the valued bits of us that have to do the changing! Our constant foe is fear. Fear of the unknown. Fear of what people will say. Fear of letting go. Fear of insecurity. If we wobble in our perception of God as a loving Father, that fear will consume us. Although the bulk of this book is about analysis, about the nuts and bolts of what is going on in the world, at its centre, and at the centre of the process I am inviting you to join, there, is and always must be, reflection on the love of God.

In the diagram you will notice that around reflection on the love of God are arranged four other activities. The first is analysis. If we are going to take the kairos seriously we have to take the facts seriously. The facts are sacred. They are part of God's revelation of himself, something that many agnostic scientists half-perceive. But facts don't exist in a vacuum. What makes a fact sacred is how it is used, how it helps to build up a part of the truth.

And that is the key point. For if the kairos is not discerned in and through truth, it is not the kairos; it is someone's prejudice, or bandwagon, or manipulation. Testing the truth, struggling with the facts and the meaning, the pattern, they point to, is therefore a central part of discovering the purposes of God in the history of our time.

It is, though, a difficult business. It has to be worked at and sweated over. What I have been able to offer in this book is only a first taste. It will not suffice anyone who takes this enterprise seriously. They will want to go on beavering away for themselves and in the process will be led into deeper truths than I have been able to share here.

But why is analysis linked to prayer in the diagram? For much the same reason that it is linked to reflection on the love of God.

The facts do not exist independently of someone to grasp them. And that someone will grasp them, will approach the truth more nearly, if he or she is aware of the blind spots and the sore places that make all perception more difficult. And the facts do not exist apart from the love of God for all his people. That is the one fact that gives all the others coherence. To put it more concretely, if we try to analyse the truth of God's world when we are consumed by hatred, anger or fear then there's not a lot of chance that we shall see much of the truth.

We have already moved from analysis to prayer. Next to being alive to the love of God, the most important part of the prayer element of the cycle is the discernment of the kairos. There is no one 'method', no guaranteed just-add-water means of discernment. For discernment is gift, it is grace. In the chapters that follow, I shall, however, suggest a kind of spiritual bi-focal: we will be looking, that is to say, at both the lovingness of God and the facts, so far as we can establish them, of the world, and will be asking where God seems to be at work. We can never be sure that we shall get it right. Discernment is always provisional—and therefore humble and tolerant.

It is made the more humble and tolerant by the fact that the second component of the prayer element consists of having a rather closer look at ourselves—both as individuals and communities. That no doubt sounds forbidding, but looking critically at ourselves, particularly at the deeper, half-submerged parts of ourselves, is only worrying or frightening if we think there is a stern judge or a harsh parent ready to take us to task for all that we discover.

There isn't.

There is a lover, a friend who desperately wants not just you and me but the whole of humankind to discover the wonders of his creation. And one of the greatest of those wonders is living together in peace and harmony and mutuality—just the things that we find most difficult while there are hurt or scarred bits of ourselves getting in the way of the kind of generous response we half-wish we were able to make.

As we shall discover in the course of the book, responding to the kairos, indeed being able to discern the kairos, requires of us an acknowledgement that we are often as much part of the problem as anyone else. And that means that before we start trying to change the world, and as we are engaged in the process of trying to change it, we do well to do whatever we can to allow those bits of us to be changed.

If we are open to the possibility, analysis and prayer lead to action. What kinds of action we shall discover as we go along.

Oscar Romero was the Archbishop of San Salvador. A champion of the poor in his country, he was assassinated in his own chapel while celebrating mass in March 1980. His funeral became a massacre when troops opened fire on the thousands of mourners.

Again, like prayer, it's horses for courses. And again like prayer, we have to find what is right for us and then get on with it. Maybe some are called to the barricades or the courtroom. Others certainly are not. Part of the process of discerning the kairos is discerning the action, the response, that is proper for us.

Notice that action too is linked to reflection on the love of God. I can best explain that with a true story. My wife works with 'peace people', helping them integrate the inner life of prayer and reflection with the outer task of working for peace. One of these people told her how shocked he had been to find within himself, at the key moment in a peace demonstration, a range of emotions that are the very antithesis of peace—hatred, anger, intolerance and violence. We need to ensure that action is never separated from reflection on the love of God.

As we go through this cycle of reflection, examination, analysis and action, we shall collect material that needs sorting out. Much of that material will be about ourselves, and, if I may speak from experience, much of it will be pretty humbling. We didn't get the analysis right. We made a mess of the action. We entirely ignored all that stuff that had seemed so important about the love of God. We feel fed up with ourselves—and, now we mention it, with the people who were supposed to be supporting us.

Yuk.

The process of appraisal may sometimes be as depressing as that. I hope not too often. The more depressing it is, the more important it is to go back to the centre of the circle. It is when we see how inadequate we are, how proud, stubborn and useless, that God can make something of us. His strength is indeed made perfect in our weakness.

I have put this cycle in terms of an individual. You or me. It is as well to get the feel for the process at that level, for it will always underlie our commitment to the kairos. But I want to put in a warning here. One of the besetting sins of western Christendom is its individualism. We tend so readily to ask ourselves: What can *I* do? Very often a better question (I would say always the prior question) is: What can *we* do? Even the great prophets of the Old Testament were, for the most part, members of prophetic communities, drawing strength and sustenance from their colleagues. Commitment to the kairos can be a demanding business. We do well to arm ourselves with the love and care of our friends.

If, then, we transpose the diagram into group terms, little need be changed. For the essential processes are likely to be needed at the individual and group levels. Individual self-examination loses none of its importance but will need to be supplemented from time to time by the group looking at itself *as a group*. The same applies to appraisal: How did the cycle go for the group as a whole?

Perhaps most thorny is the central reflection on the love of God. Some people find that so personal that it can, for them, never be shared in a group. For others, it comes most alive in the very work of sharing. It is unproductive to pontificate on what is best. I will only say that it sometimes happens that those who are at first most resistant to any group meditation or prayer end up its most ardent devotees. Clearly what matters is sensitivity to each other's needs—and a sense of humour.

A final point about the diagram and the process it represents. The key is the circularity. Like all spirituality, it is a process, a constant going-round or toing-and-froing between the inward opening to the word and Spirit of God and the outward expression of that inwardness. If the toing-and-froing is lost, we shall find not only that we burn out very fast, but that even before we do, we are beginning to lose sight of the inner nature of the kairos—which is neither more nor less than the self disclosure of God in the events of our times.

In the chapters that follow, I shall try to give you material for the working out of a spirituality of action in each of the five areas I

Ash Wednesday at Upper Hayford US Air Force base in Britain. Christians break bread and drink wine to remember the broken body and shed blood of Christ.

shall be covering. But a word of caution: in the format of a book, the analytical necessarily takes priority. I can make suggestions for the other parts of the process, but they can be only the lightest touches. For to do more would be to refuse to take you and your situation, with all its particularities, sufficiently seriously. You know where you—and your community—are. I don't. I can help you think out the issues. I can point you to helpful biblical material. I can suggest how you might spend time in prayer. I can, sometimes, point you to relevant action ... But in the end, you are on your own.

So back to reflection on the love of God.

# Chapter One
# POVERTY

## REFLECTION ON THE LOVE OF GOD

READ EZEKIEL 36:25–30

I shall pour clean water over you and you will be cleansed; I shall cleanse you of all your defilement and all your idols. I shall give you a new heart, and put a new spirit in you; I shall remove the heart of stone from your bodies and give you a heart of flesh instead. I shall put my spirit in you, and make you keep my laws and sincerely respect my observances. You will live in the land which I gave your ancestors. You shall be my people and I will be your God. I shall rescue you from all your defilement. I shall summon the corn and make it plentiful, and no more bring famines on you. I shall increase the yield of fruit trees and fields so that you will no longer have the ignominy of famine among the nations.

This is a summary of the covenant between Israel and Yahweh. The phrase 'You shall be my people and I will be your God' recurs constantly throughout the Old Testament as the essence of what it means to be the chosen people of God. On the side of the people, it implies total loyalty to Yahweh and the abandonment of the false gods to which they were constantly attracted. From the side of Yahweh, it offers peace and prosperity—land, rain, harvests and victory over the neighbouring tribes.

The history of Israel is the history of this Covenant. They break it constantly, either by pursuing the false gods and thereby calling into question the power of Yahweh, or by refusing to work out the terms of the covenant in their relationships with each other.

Yet the love of God is prior. It is he that initiates the covenant. It is he who constantly recalls Israel to its terms. It is he who will not let go. Finally, as we shall see below, it is he who has to start all over again.

READ LEVITICUS 25:8–19

'You are to count seven weeks of years—seven times seven years, that is to say a period of seven weeks of years, forty-nine years. And on the tenth day of the seventh month you shall sound the trumpet; on the Day of Atonement you shall sound the trumpet throughout the land. You will declare this fiftieth year sacred and proclaim the liberation of all the inhabitants of the land. This is to be a jubilee for you; each of you will return to his ancestral home, each to his own clan. This fiftieth year is to be a jubilee year for you: you will not sow, you will not harvest the ungathered corn, you will not gather from the untrimmed vine. The jubilee is to be a holy thing to you, you will eat what comes from the fields.

'In this year of jubilee each of you is to return to his ancestral home. If you buy or sell with your neighbour, let no one wrong his brother. If you buy from your neighbour, this must take into account the number of years since the jubilee: according to the number of productive years he will fix the price. The greater the number of years, the higher shall be the price demanded; the less the number of years, the greater the reduction, for what he is selling you is a certain number of harvests. Let none of you wrong his neighbour, but fear your God; I am Yahweh your God.

'You must put my laws and customs into practice; you must keep them, practise them; and so you shall be secure in your possession of the land. The land will give its fruit, you will eat your fill and live in security.'

In the religious consciousness of the people of Israel, the implications of the covenant were gradually worked out and incorporated in formal legislation. Though much of that had to do with worship and the details of liturgy and family life, it is clear that, from surprisingly early, it was recognised that the covenant-love of Yahweh had immmediate implications for the conduct of social and economic relationships.

The Year of the Jubilee was one such. In it slaves are to be freed, debts forgiven (made more explicit in Deut. 15:1–11) and the land allowed to rest. Above all, the people must examine afresh their way of doing business: 'no one must wrong his brother'.

For the Covenant can only bring the material and social benefits that Yahweh has promised his people as signs of his love if they play their part.

READ AMOS 5:21—6.7

I hate and despise your feasts,
I take no pleasure in your solemn festivals.
When you offer me holocausts....
I reject your oblations,
and refuse to look at your sacrifices of fattened cattle.
Let me have no more of the din of your chanting,
no more of your strumming on harps.
But let justice flow like water,
and integrity like an unfailing stream.
Did you bring me sacrifice and oblation in the wilderness
for all those forty years, House of Israel?
Now you must shoulder Sakkuth your king
and Kaiwan your god,
those idols you have made for yourselves;
for I mean to take you far beyond Damascus into exile,
says Yahweh—God of Sabaoth is his name.
Woe to those ensconced so snugly in Zion
and to those who feel so safe on the mountain of Samaria,
those famous men of this first of nations

to whom the House of Israel goes as client.
Make a journey to Calneh and look,
go on from there to Hamath the great,
then down to Gath in Philistia.
Are they any better off than these kingdoms?
Is their territory larger than yours?
You think to defer the day of misfortune,
but you hasten the reign of violence.
Lying on ivory beds
and sprawling on their divans,
they dine on lambs from the flock,
and stall-fattened veal;
they bawl to the sound of the harp,
they invent new instruments of music like David,
they drink wine by the bowlful,
and use the finest oil for anointing themselves,
but about the ruin of Joseph they do not care at all.
That is why they will be the first to be exiled;
the sprawlers' revelry is over.

The people do not play their part. They allow religion to become formalised, a matter of the lips rather than the heart. They continue to pursue the false gods. They revel in luxury and imagine that they can ensure their own safety.

It is vital to read Amos's scathing denunciation in the light of the opening of this part of the record of his ministry. It can be found in the first couplet of chapter 3: 'Listen, sons of Israel, to this oracle Yahweh speaks against you, against the whole family I brought out of the land of Egypt: You alone, of all the families of the earth, have I acknowledged ...'

READ JEREMIAH 31:31–34

See, the days are coming—it is Yahweh who speaks—when I will make a new covenant with the House of Israel (and the House of Judah), but not a covenant like the one I made with their ancestors on the day I took them by the hand to bring them out of the land of Egypt. They broke that covenant of mine, so I had to show them who was master. It is Yahweh who speaks. No, this is the covenant I will make with the House of Israel when those days arrive—it is Yahweh who speaks. Deep within them I will plant my Law, writing it on their hearts. Then I will be their God and they shall be my people. There will be no further need for neighbour to try to teach neighbour, or brother to say to brother, 'Learn to know Yahweh!' No, they will all know me, the least no less than the greatest—it is Yahweh who speaks—since I will forgive their iniquity and never call their sin to mind.

We are at the centre of the religion of the Old Testament. The old covenant between Yahweh and his people has been broken, again and again. By defying the terms of the covenant, especially by failing to recognise Yahweh as the only God, the people of Israel have made the covenant inoperable. So Yahweh is going to have to start again. This time he will 'plant the Law deep within them'. It will no longer be a forced, a learned response, but a joyful reaction to the love of God.

The new covenant will come out of the forgiveness for the past failures. Yahweh's graciousness will call forth a spontaneous commitment from the people. The dead hand of the Law will be replaced by the inspiration of love.

READ LUKE 15:14–24

'When he had spent it all, that country experienced a severe famine, and now he began to feel the pinch, so he hired himself out to one of the local inhabitants who put him on his farm to feed the pigs. And he would willingly have filled his belly with the husks the pigs were eating but no one offered him anything. Then he came to his senses and said, "How many of my father's paid servants have more food than they want, and here am I dying of hunger! I will leave this place and go to my father and say: Father, I have sinned against heaven and against you; I no longer deserve to be called your son; treat me as one of your paid servants." So he left the place and went back to his father.

'While he was still a long way off, his father saw him and was moved with pity. He ran to the boy, clasped him in his arms and kissed him tenderly. Then his son said, "Father, I have sinned against heaven and against you. I no longer deserve to be called your son." But the father said to his servants, "Quick! Bring out the best robe and put it on him; put a ring on his finger and sandals on his feet. Bring the calf we have been fattening, and kill it; we are going to have a feast, a celebration, because this son of mine was dead and has come back to life; he was lost and is found." And they began to celebrate.'

The Old Testament covenant is replaced by the notion of the kingdom of God. And like the covenant, the initiative of the kingdom is God's. It is his kingdom, not ours. It is given by God, not built by men and women. But men and women have to decide where they stand. Are they prepared to become part of the kingdom—or do they want to go on making excuses for having nothing to do with it? In Mark 10:17–22, we find just how hard that choice can be.

As we read these passages, we might reflect on four things:

☐ Do we allow Christian morality to become a dead, juridical 'law'? Or do we keep alive an ethic that springs from loving thankfulness for the goodness of God?

☐ Do we tend to divorce 'religion' from the whole of life, including politics and economics—not in theory and concept, but in the stuff of how we actually spend our time and order our priorities?

☐ What are our favourite false gods?

☐ Where in our lives do we find the tension between the values of the kingdom (you might want to re-read the Sermon on the Mount) and the values that come most naturally to us?

As we work on these questions, it is important not to flagellate ourselves with guilt. God goes on loving us whatever—and he loves us with great graciousness when we grapple with the things that get in the way of our growth towards him.

It will be helpful to work on these questions at both the individual level, and as a group. If you cannot meet in a group it is still worth asking these questions of groups that you are a member of, and especially the church of which you are a member. Just as the point is not to judge yourself harshly as an individual, so in the group work, you are not being asked to judge the group or the church, but to try to look at it lovingly from the perspective of the biblical record.

## ANALYSIS

According to the World Bank, 800 million people live in absolute poverty, that is, 'they lack the basic necessities of a human existence'. It is hard for us to understand either the numbers involved or what it means to live in absolute poverty.

First, the numbers. If the poor of the world held hands, they would make a line that would extend to the surface of the moon. And back. Twice. Unless things change radically, it is expected that by the end of this century the line will grow out to the moon again.

What does poverty really mean?

The most common way of comparing levels of affluence and levels of poverty is by contrasting income per head. Thus in the United States the average annual income per head is $16,690; in India it is $270; and in Ethiopia it is $110. These figures do not tell us very much. We need to try to get nearer to the realities of people's lives.

First, however, a word of warning. We can compare figures of life expectancy, literacy, access to health care and other indicators of levels of living. That tells us something—and such figures appear in the table on page 24. They tell us nothing, however, of the human emotions that lie behind those figures. It is sometimes said: 'Oh, they're used to having their children die—or going hungry or inadequately clothed. They don't notice it like we would.' Anyone who has had the privilege of living among poor people knows that to be rubbish—and racist rubbish at that. I have witnessed terrible grief at the death of a child, albeit the seventh in a desperately poor household. I have seen children fight to kill for the sake of vegetable peelings in a dustbin, 'a little something to

## POVERTY INDICATORS

| Country | Life Expectancy at Birth (male 1985) | Infant Mortality Rate (per 1,000 1985) | People per Doctor 1981 | Daily Calorie Intake per Head |
|---|---|---|---|---|
| ETHIOPIA | 43 | 168 | 88,720 | 1681 |
| BANGLADESH | 50 | 123 | 9,700 | 1899 |
| MOZAMBIQUE | 45 | 123 | 37,000 | 1678 |
| INDIA | 57 | 89 | 3,700 | 2189 |
| EGYPT | 59 | 63 | 760 | 3263 |
| PHILIPPINES | 61 | 48 | 6,710 | 2341 |
| ZIMBABWE | 55 | 77 | 7,100 | 2054 |
| CHILE | 67 | 22 | n/a | 2602 |
| PORTUGAL | 71 | 19 | 500 | 3161 |
| GREECE | 72 | 16 | 400 | 3721 |
| UNITED KINGDOM | 72 | 9 | 680 | 3131 |
| SWITZERLAND | 73 | 8 | 390 | 3432 |
| UNITED STATES | 72 | 11 | 500 | 3663 |

quieten the stomach', as the victor put it. I have seen the look on a wife's face when her husband comes home in the evening having again failed to find work. The figures tell a human story: they have to be read with what David Jenkins calls statistical compassion.

One way of picking up much of the statistical and some of the human information is to compare life expectancy at birth. If we ignore China and Vietnam (because the figures are frankly unreliable) then we find that the life expectancy at birth in the remaining thirty-five poorest countries is around fifty-two years. That is twenty-four years shorter than for the eighteen rich western countries. Just what that means is hard for us to grasp. Try going through your circle of friends or any reasonably representative group of your community and see how many would not be there if everyone died at the age of fifty-two. You might like to bring a combination of 'statistical compassion' and imagination to bear on the other figures in the table above.

For when we talk of 800 million people living in absolute poverty those are some—but only some—of the dimensions we mean.

There are others—fear, insecurity, superstition, anxiety, loneliness—which no figures can capture. Certainly there is a positive side: laughter, communal sharing, often a firm social structure, and a fatalism that protects people from despair or anger. People, however, vote with their feet. They are leaving the rural areas of the developing world and moving to the towns in search—often in vain—of something better: a living wage, a chance for their children, relief from the vice-like grip of the seasons, a chance, however remote, of a lucky break to a decent standard of living through winning the national lottery, or fighting their way up the commercial or political ladder.

## WHY ARE POOR PEOPLE POOR?

There are no easy answers to such a huge question. The reasons for the poverty of slum-dwellers in Sao Paul, Brazil are obviously quite different from the reasons for the poverty of landless peasants in Rajasthan, India.

Recognising that, I want none the less to highlight a number of factors that are common to a large proportion of poor people wherever they are.

Water has always been a symbol of life. In the Old Testament, God promised to cleanse his people with fresh water. And yet only one home in seven worldwide has a piped water supply. This tap on a water-seller's cart in Gujarat is firmly padlocked.

## 1. The poverty of the natural environment

The majority of the 800 million live in rural areas, so we must begin there. Many of the rural poor live in a natural environment that is almost unimaginably harsh—on desert fringes, with low and irregular rainfall; on savannahs where the soils are weak and easily reduced to a wholly infertile laterite; on plains that are fertile but subject to frequent and destructive flooding; on steep hillsides that quickly erode if tree cover is removed.

The natural hostility of these environments is unleashed as greater demands are made upon them. Each can support small numbers of people who understand the environment and adopt a lifestyle that works with rather than against the logic of that environment. As population pressure builds up—either from natural increase or from migration as 'excess' population is forced out of more desirable locations, so these environments suffer a cycle of decline that makes the acutest poverty inevitable. Trees are cut: nutrients are leached from the soil: soil washes away: so more trees are cut: firewood becomes scarce: so trees are cut further away.

Many of these harsh environments can be made productive, even with the higher populations they have to support. That, however, involves a huge technical leap—the application of fertiliser;

Deforestation is a major cause of soil erosion. At the beginning of this century, 40 per cent of Ethiopian land was forest. Today, only 3 per cent remains. Stripping the land in this way prepared the way for the Ethiopian famine in the late 1980s.

the growing of improved pastures; the limitation of stock; the replanting of trees; most radical of all, the adoption of irrigation. Poor people cannot do that alone. They need help, on a massive scale. And yet many official (that is, government to government) donor aid agencies give much more aid to richer farmers growing export crops like tobacco or rubber or cocoa than they do to poor peasants in harsh lands growing their own food.

The difficulties of such people are aggravated when newcomers move into the land. Most of these newcomers are people who have been made landless elsewhere. They have been forced out by high rents, or by landowners who terminate tenancies, or by litigation—or, for example in Brazil and the Philippines, by agribusinesses growing export crops. In the developing world, landlessness is a desperate condition. Without access to either land, or regular employment, people go hungry.

**2. The inadequacy of the social environment**

Their lot is made worse by the social environment in which the rural poor find themselves. Few government services like health and education reach them. Many surveys show that when such services are available, the poorest tend to use them last. For example, even if education is free—and often in practice some cash outlay is involved in sending a child to school, if only for books and uniform—the household may not be able to survive without the labour of even young children. For they are part of the family's life support system. In the brass industry in South India, for example, children of six are employed in the workshops and their earnings may make the difference between their siblings being fed or going hungry.

It is the women who suffer most. In many cultures in the developing world, women are regarded as unclean and/or inferior. Yet, especially in the rural areas, they do the work that enables the family to survive. They grow the food. They fetch the water and fuel. They do the marketing (especially in West Africa and the Caribbean). And of course they rear the children who often appear in quick succession. In many parts of Africa and Latin America it is the women who produce the beer—for the men to drink! One can say this is their traditional role. What is much less traditional, however, is that they now have to do this alone, unsupported by their menfolk who are often in town looking for a job. In parts of sub Saharan Africa as many as 70 per cent of rural households are headed by women. The physical and emotional wear hardly needs description.

The women, moreover, tend to be locked into their rural prison.

Juvenile brass-workers in Madras. In the world's poorest countries, young children work long, exhausting hours to supplement their family's income.

This woman, from Tigray, Ethiopia, is doing an everyday job in the Third World. She is carrying a heavy earthenware pot, full of water, over the miles that separate her nearest water supply from her home.

It is the men who escape—to hunt for work in the towns. There they find themselves competing in a buyers' market, for there are many more job seekers than there are jobs. Urban unemployment rates of over 30 per cent are thus not uncommon. With no dole, the unemployed resort to a wide variety of activities in the euphemistically entitled 'informal' sector—from legal but degrading occupations like sifting garbage, to illegal and even more degrading activities like procuring, prostitution, theft and racketeering.

The grim truth is that this situation looks like getting worse. According to World Bank estimates, the labour force in the poorest countries is set to grow by 2.6 per cent per annum between now and the end of the century. There is no likelihood at all that the number of jobs will grow at that pace. (It is an interesting contrast that in two of the richest European countries, West Germany and Switzerland, the labour force will actually contract: for 'guest-workers' from Northern Africa and Turkey will be sent home.) Yet, so low is the quality of life in the rural areas, that the urban population in the poorest countries will double in the next thirteen years. What that means for the quality of life in those towns is best left to the imagination.

## THE ROLE OF GOVERNMENT

It is a perfectly reasonable response to the facts so far presented to ask what the governments of poor countries are doing to solve the problems we have identified. In few countries do governments set out deliberately to impoverish their own citizens. True, some persecute minorities—Indians in Guatemala; Muslims in the Philippines; 'hill tribes' in Bangladesh—with the result that such minorities are kept in conditions of extreme poverty, and no less extreme fear.

More commonly, governments respond to political pressures in ways which may have, as an unintended consequence, damaging effects on the poor. Here are some examples:

**1.** Keeping down the prices paid to farmers for food: this may help the urban poor, but impoverishes the food producers—who are usually much more numerous.

**2.** Taxing crops that small farmers produce for export: like cocoa, tea or coffee. Sometimes the rate of tax on such crops is higher than that paid by middle class professionals, like doctors or teachers.

**3.** Raising minimum wage rates to an unrealistic level and thus reducing the number of jobs available.

**4.** Adopting policies that displace 'informal' jobs—for example, a

Poverty in Lima, Peru. Absolute poverty means one pair of shoes shared between a family, and long hours of hard labour for little pay. Absolute poverty means no local doctor. Absolute poverty turns an illness such as diarrhoea into a death sentence.

supermarket kills the trade of street vendors; the importing of plastic buckets kills the trade of local tinsmiths.

**5.** Keeping exchange rates too high and thus hampering the growth of exports and encouraging imports—both at the cost of jobs at home.

**6.** Spending too much on bloated and inefficient public services (which tend to be politically powerful); and on the armed forces (which tend to be politically crucial).

**7.** Allowing the over-generous incentives given to multinational corporations to get them to operate in developing countries: for example, tax holidays and subsidies.

When all this is said, however, the fact remains that in very many developing countries, and supremely in sub-Saharan Africa, even the wisest and fairest government would find that there is simply not enough money or trained personnel to give everyone a decent education, adequate health care, a job or access to land, clean water and an assured supply of food at affordable prices.

At the margin, a straight choice has to be made—better roads in the capital or a minimal road in an outlying, thinly populated, politically weak area? More places at university (at $10,000 per student per year) for the children of articulate urban middle class parents—or a hundred primary school places (at $100 per year) in a remote village?

Politics raises its head when all such issues have to be faced. Poor people do not generally deliver much political clout; inevitably they find political choices biased against them. Smart hospitals are built in town while rural health clinics have no drugs. Loans are available for property speculation in the smart suburbs, but not for small scale agriculture. Trade unions are kept weak or under tight control so that they cannot press for improved conditions.

Yes, there *is* political manipulation, corruption, exploitation and appalling cruelty in the developing world. It is romantic or self-deluding to deny that. And that *is* a major cause of mass poverty and human degradation. To a degree that we are reluctant to admit, however, it is modelled, consciously or unconsciously, on the 'Christian' West. Before we condemn the moral turpitude of the wealthy in India or Mexico or the Ivory Coast, then, we had better look more carefully at our own. We shall find the kairos is not only a moment of opportunity. It is also a moment of judgment.

## THE INTERNATIONAL ENVIRONMENT

A message intended for would-be importers in Ghana.

Before we look at the impact of our culture on the poor of the world, it is important to put it into some kind of perspective. I have

Exports
GAIN!
Imports
DRAIN!
AFROMEDIA

The world of international finance seems a million miles away from the lives of ordinary people, but the two are directly connected. The Great Depression, symbolised by the crash on Wall Street in 1929, created impoverishment on a vast scale in America.

suggested that most of the poorest live in the rural areas, producing (sometimes exclusively) for their own subsistence. The extent to which the combined effect of all rich countries on their way of life explains their poverty is much disputed. At one extreme, people argue that the life of Saharan nomads or Kalahari bushmen remains quite untouched by the issues we shall be raising in this section. At the other end of the scale, the lot of tea pickers in Kenya or small scale cocoa farmers in Ghana may be affected by what we pay for tea or cocoa. (Though the effect may be less immediate and direct than it appears to be at first glance.)

Between and underneath these two extremes lies a much deeper debate about the effect of western culture and especially capitalism on the rural areas of the developing world. It is easier to summarise the questions raised in the debate than the myriad answers that anthropologists and sociologists have produced from field research. Is capitalism really destroying traditional forms of peasant life—and if it is, who is gaining and who is losing? And are the losers worse off than they would have been under the old forms of organisation?

There is and can be no one answer to that. There *are* examples of peasant communities being destroyed by 'modernisation' and many people being forced off the land and obliged to become (underemployed) wage labourers. And one can sometimes trace the links back to western corporations or consumers. The cattle industry in Brazil; the sugar industry in Peru; the tea industry in Sri Lanka are three very different examples.

Equally, however, one can find examples of capitalist penetration of peasant agriculture that seems to have brought great benefits—for example, the cocoa industry in Nigeria and Ghana in the 1950s and the oil palm industry in Malaysia in the 1970s.

These are deep and troubled waters, and although enormously important in the long-run, they have to remain beyond the scope of our present undertaking. For there are many more, direct and *reversible* ways in which our societies contribute to the maintenance of the poverty of the poor.

## 1. Aid

Most people in the rich North think that the only relationship between themselves and the poor in the South is the aid that the rich countries give to the poor. Certainly that is not negligible, but it is probably the least significant point. Let us look at it first to get it out of the way.

Aid has a role to play, especially in enabling the rural poor to make productive the difficult environment in which many of them

CORY
PRESIDENT

A Philippine crowd calls for President Marcos to step down following a rigged result in 1986's presidential elections. Following his brutal and oppressive 21-year rule, Marcos was replaced by Corazon Aquino.

live. Aid *can* be effective. And we are told that aid programmes are becoming ever more so. Is that true?

*Not* in terms of volume. The official *UN* target for government aid is 0.7 per cent of national income. The US gives 0.29 per cent; the UK 0.32 per cent; Canada 0.35 per cent; Australia 0.36 per cent. *Some* countries do much better: Sweden 1.1 per cent; Denmark 0.98 per cent.

*Not* in terms of quality. Most countries tie their aid to purchases of goods and services in their own countries—so about 70 per cent of British bilateral aid must be used to buy British goods; and about the same proportion of American aid is committed to the purchase of goods made in the USA. This not only reduces the value of the aid (since cheaper tractors or drugs are likely to be available elsewhere); more destructively, it means that an inappropriate technology tends to be associated with aid (since the *only* technology available in the UK or the US or Canada is likely to be unsuitable in India or Bangladesh with their very different conditions).

*Not* in terms of responsiveness to need. Aid is used as a tool of foreign policy. The needs of poor people are only one, usually rather a minor, consideration. The UK gives ten times as much (per head of the population) to Turkey, a NATO ally and a semi-industrialised country as it does to Bangladesh, a former

**AID TO LDCs**
as percentage of National Income

| | 1965 | 1975 | 1986 |
|---|---|---|---|
| IRELAND | 0.00 (0.00) | 0.09 (n/a) | 0.28 (0.05) |
| ITALY | n/a (0.04) | 0.16 (0.24) | 0.40 (0.12) |
| NETHERLANDS | 0.36 (0.08) | 0.61 (0.24) | 1.00 (0.27) |
| FRANCE | 0.76 (0.12) | 0.62 (0.10) | 0.72 (0.14) |
| AUSTRALIA | 0.53 (0.08) | 0.65 (0.10) | 0.49 (0.05) |
| GERMANY | 0.40 (0.14) | 0.40 (0.12) | 0.43 (0.14) |
| SWEDEN | 0.19 (0.07) | 0.82 (0.41) | 0.88 (0.31) |
| CANADA | 0.19 (0.10) | 0.34 (0.24) | 0.48 (0.15) |
| UNITED STATES | 0.58 (0.26) | 0.27 (0.08) | 0.23 (0.04) |
| UNITED KINGDOM | 0.47 (0.23) | 0.39 (0.11) | 0.33 (0.09) |

(Aid to poorest 36 countries in brackets)

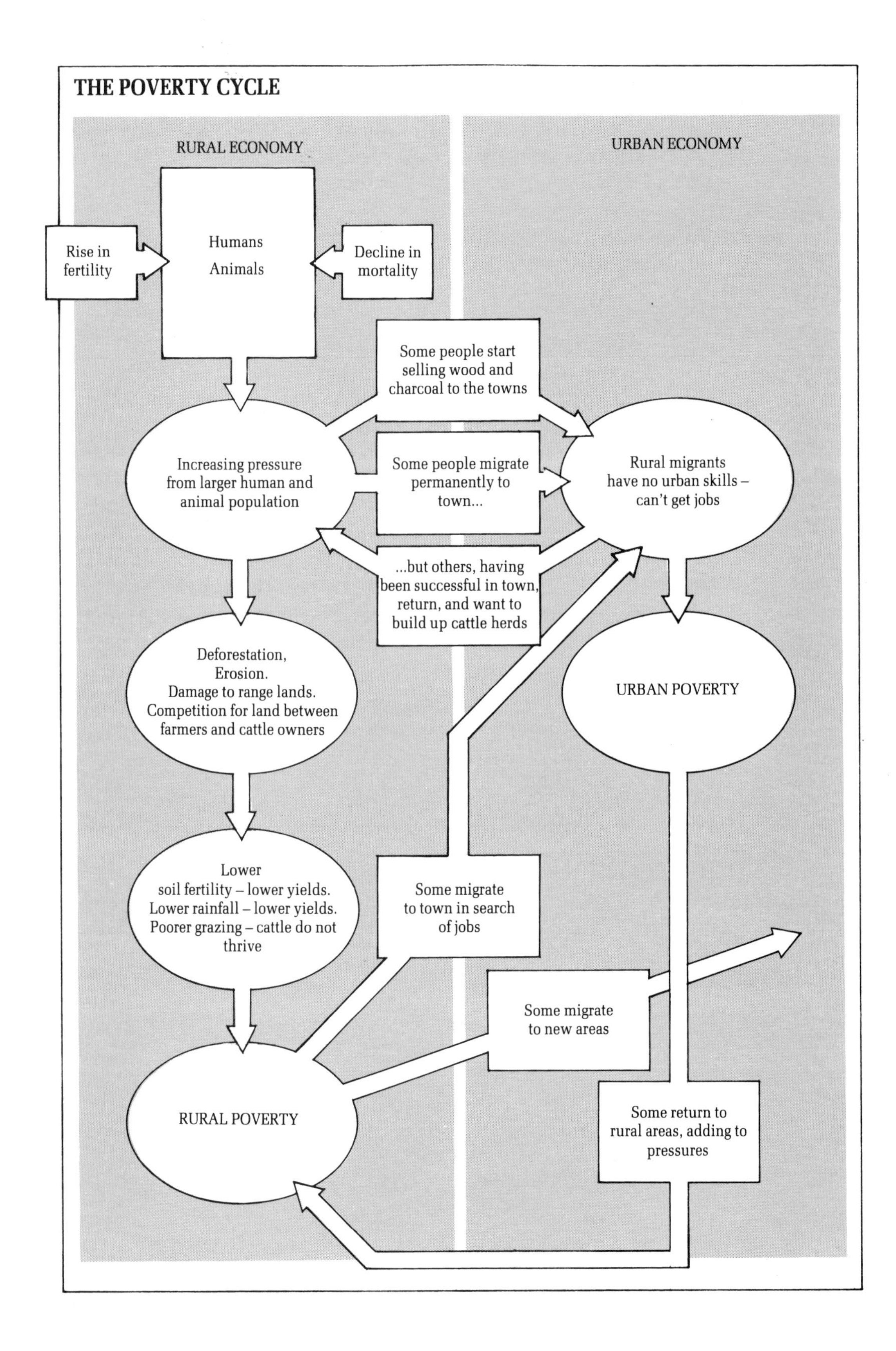
THE POVERTY CYCLE
RURAL ECONOMY
URBAN ECONOMY
Rise in fertility
Humans
Animals
Decline in mortality
Some people start selling wood and charcoal to the towns
Increasing pressure from larger human and animal population
Some people migrate permanently to town...
Rural migrants have no urban skills – can't get jobs
...but others, having been successful in town, return, and want to build up cattle herds
Deforestation, Erosion. Damage to range lands. Competition for land between farmers and cattle owners
URBAN POVERTY
Lower soil fertility – lower yields. Lower rainfall – lower yields. Poorer grazing – cattle do not thrive
Some migrate to town in search of jobs
Some migrate to new areas
RURAL POVERTY
Some return to rural areas, adding to pressures

colony. The US gives generously to Costa Rica and El Salvador, middle income countries that are strategically important, but meanly to some of the poorest countries in the world—Chad, Mali, Tanzania.

But what of emergency aid? What of Ethiopia and Mozambique in 1984/85? Is that not a triumph of sorts? Yes—and no. Emergency aid, both official and voluntary, has a role to play, and no one would wish to deny Bob Geldof and his associates the accolade of a job well done. After a slow start, even western governments, under strong pressure from public opinion, provided resources and logistical support that could not come from voluntary agencies alone.

And yet ... two things need to be said. First, the signs of famine were clear long before either voluntary agencies (with one or two exceptions) or governments began to move. That is not untypical, especially in famines (as opposed to earthquakes or typhoons where the evidence is unquestionable). Second, and much more important, the level of liaison and co-ordination on the ground was, in the case of Ethiopia, and is typically in all such crises, so poor as seriously to jeopardise the efficiency of the operation. And there is good reason for that. Each agency wants the high prestige, high profile PR project. Each agency wants *its* pictures of *its* staff delivering *its* food to '*its*' victims. The competition, jostling, manipulation and skulduggery is as disturbing as it is inevitable—as long as we, the public, need that kind of publicity to galvanise us to generosity.

Disasters will no doubt occur. Whether famine need ever recur is a much more debatable question. This is not the place to review at any length the growing literature on the causes of famine. One point, however, is critical for the rest of our discussion. Famine is the result of poverty. There is always some food somewhere close to the disaster area (as there was in Ethiopia in 1985). What is lacking is the means to buy it.

In that way, there is a direct connection between famine and the five more significant points that we move to now.

## 2. International prices

Like any individual, a country can afford to spend only what it can earn or borrow. It earns by selling what it produces. And the value of that produce is determined by the quantity and the price.

That is why the chart on page 40 is not just a bit of economics. It is a demonstration of sin.

It shows that the prices of the raw materials (excluding oil) produced by the developing world have fallen unsteadily but certainly since the 1950s. In the unemotional tones of the World Bank:

> For the first time in recent history, practically all commodity groups experienced price declines 1984-86 ... In 1985, the World Bank's index of 33 non-fuel primary commodity prices ... fell to its lowest level in nine years.'

The reasons are easily explained.

☐ Demand has not grown fast, especially for things like cotton, wool, hard fibres and copper, where new technology has produced 'man-made' substitutes.

☐ Because they can produce little else, more and more countries are persuaded (sometimes by the World Bank; sometimes by government donors; sometimes by western corporations) to increase production of raw materials.

In 1950 there were only three major exporters of cocoa. There are now thirteen. Malaysia led the world in the export of palm oil. Then Latin American countries started producing it on a large scale. The Prime Minister of Malaysia said in 1986 that he never expected to see the price of Malaysian palm oil recover to the levels of the mid-seventies. At the same time, he announced a major

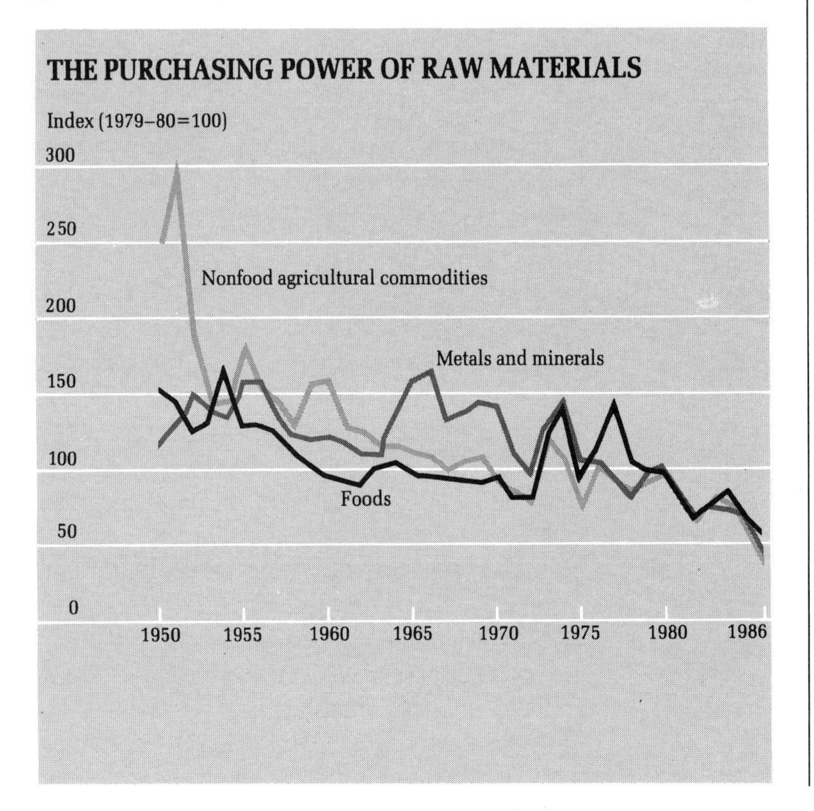

delay in programmes aimed at raising the living standards of the Bumiputra, 'the sons of the soil'.

□ Third, and most damnable, the increased supply of cheap exports of agricultural surpluses from the US and EEC has spoilt the markets for Third World countries. Chad, one of the poorest countries in the world, is a mordant example.

In February 1986, Chad was recovering from the famine of 1983–85. Chad exports cotton—and is therefore heavily reliant on the price her cotton fetches on world markets for importing bare essentials like oil, pharmaceuticals and spare parts. In late 1985, she had been getting 1400 francs CFA per pound for her cotton—a profitable price. But then two things happened. China started exporting cotton on a large scale and the US announced that American exports of cotton would be subsidised in order to protect the incomes of American farmers. The prices of Chad's cotton fell to 700 francs CFA by February 1986—and to 500 frances CFA by April. In less than seven months, Chad's export earnings had declined by nearly two-thirds.

If it were the case that the prices of goods most developing countries import were falling at roughly the same rate, the one would offset the other. But look again at the chart on page 40 and ask yourself in which direction the prices of the following products, all typically imported by the Third World, have moved since 1950—a tractor; a bag of fertiliser; a typewriter.

It is this discrepancy between the prices of exports and the prices of imports that is the most fundamental cause of the poverty of the Third World. When we buy, we pay what the market will bear. When we sell, we charge what will give a satisfactory standard of living. The contrast is startling. No one asks a Ghanian cocoa farmer what it cost him to produce a ton of cocoa beans. We pay what will clear the market. But when he wants to buy an X-ray machine or a lorry or a lathe, we demand a price that reflects the cost of production; the cost, that is, of maintaining our standard of living.

The effect is shattering. Even in the relatively short period 1980–85, Zambia found that the purchasing price of her copper (her only significant export) had declined 28 per cent.

### 3. Trade

Is there a way out? The conventional wisdom is that poor countries should process their raw materials and export manufactured goods rather than commodities. But as soon as they become successful at that, they find that the rich countries do not want their exports—

because they threaten jobs at home. They therefore keep them out—by tariffs; or quotas; or 'voluntary' restrictions; or bogus health regulations; or threats of counter measures. Some of these restrictions are illegal; but how can Mauritius or Bangladesh enforce international law against Germany or UK or US? Here's a telling example.

Bangladesh grows cotton and has traditionally exported it either raw or as woven cloth. In an effort to create jobs and earn more foreign exchange, the government of Bangladesh invested heavily in modern shirt-making factories and began to export shirts to the EEC and North America. In Canada, a government enquiry was ordered when Bangladesh had captured less than ¾ per cent of the domestic market; and she was obliged to agree to 'voluntary' cutbacks when the figure rose to 1 per cent.

In the UK, the story is similar—initial success, followed by pressure from the domestic industry causing the British government to monitor and then reduce Bangladeshi exports, even though they account for only a tiny fraction of the British market.

It is estimated that the restrictions imposed by the rich countries cost 40,000 jobs in Bangladesh and over $1 million of export earnings—each working day.

It is hard to exaggerate the scale and significance of these restrictions. The table below shows that over the last five years the

**BARRIERS TO TRADE**

THE PROPORTION OF RICH COUNTRIES' IMPORTS FROM DEVELOPING COUNTRIES AFFECTED BY NON-TARIFF BARRIERS

| | 1981 | 1986 |
|---|---|---|
| ORE AND METALS | 8.6 | 12.8 |
| Iron & Steel | 24.8 | 54.6 |
| Non-ferrous metals | 6.1 | 6.4 |
| Chemicals | 11.4 | 12.6 |
| MANUFACTURERS | 31.3 | 31.0 |
| Leather | 9.9 | 9.9 |
| Textiles, yarn, fabrics | 57.6 | 61.4 |
| Clothing | 77.1 | 77.9 |
| Footwear | 71.0 | 27.0 |

extent of these 'voluntary' restrictions has increased substantially and they now cover a large part of the exports of developing countries. (As well as 'voluntary export restrictions', the table includes other devices to keep out Third World imports—from price control to quotas, but does not include some of the more exotic lengths to which rich countries sometimes resort, the most famous of which was the French insistence that all Japanese VCRs be cleared through the remote and understaffed customs shed in Poitiers!)

It comes as no surprise to find that rich countries protect themselves much more vigorously from the exports of Third World countries than from each other's exports. In the general case of manufacturers, for example, on which the poor countries depend critically for creating jobs, the degree of protection from the poor countries' exports is almost double that from other rich countries. You scratch my back and I'll scratch yours.

### 4. Debt

If you put the last three sections together, you can see the nature of the problems faced by the Third World. They get less and less for the raw materials they sell. They find it harder and harder to sell manufactures. What little aid is available goes, in general, in the wrong form to the less poor countries ... So what to do?

That problem seemed soluble when western banks were flush with the unspent earnings deposited by the oil producers. The bankers were willing to lend, some would say over-willing, to Third World governments who would guarantee repayment.

Coincidentally, the borrowers were able to go on importing from the rich countries when they, the rich countries, were faced with recession. On one calculation, a million jobs in Europe were saved by the Third World borrowers.

So what went wrong? Several things:

☐ Raw material prices dropped sharply: there was less money to repay the debt.

☐ Interest rates rose, especially 1980–82 (see the chart on page 44).

☐ The value of the dollar rose in the early Reagan years.

☐ Some of the borrowers, notably Poland and Argentina, did not use the borrowed money wisely.

☐ Too much was borrowed—and lent.

By 1982 it was clear that a major financial crisis threatened. It was averted by a mixture of skill, luck and arm-twisting, and the subsequent fall of the dollar and of interest rates has helped defuse the crisis.

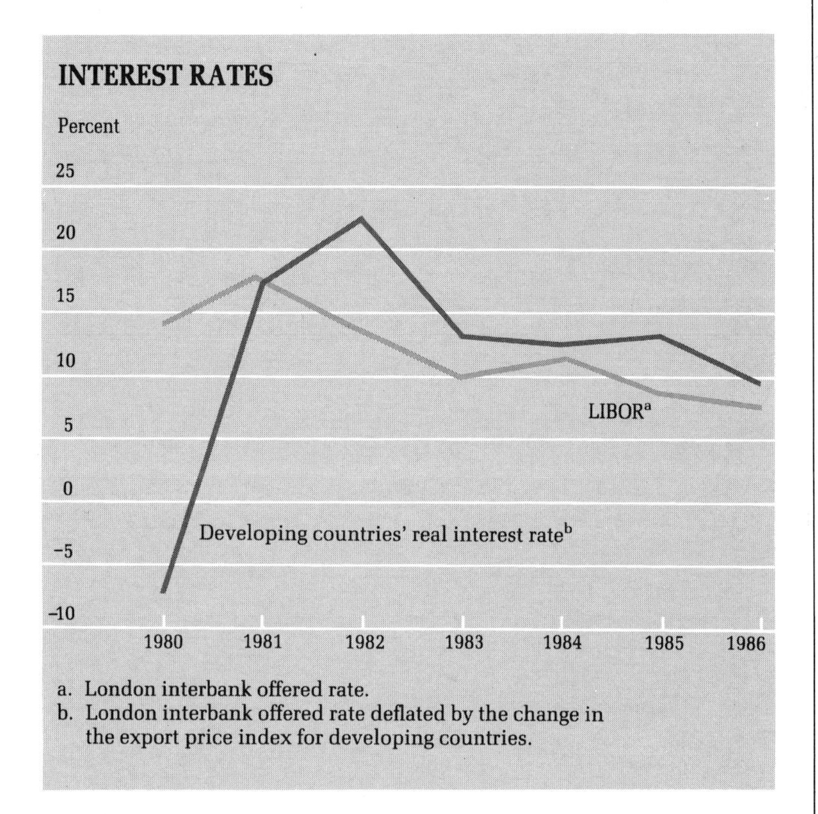


a. London interbank offered rate.
b. London interbank offered rate deflated by the change in the export price index for developing countries.

That does not change the basic fact: many developing countries are now so deeply in debt that it is inconceivable that they will ever repay their loans in full.

Yet the pressure on them to do so remains intense. That pressure is usually mediated through the banker's bank, the International Monetary Fund. It has tended to take a very hard line with countries wishing to borrow from it, insisting on a package of measures that have had serious effects on the poor:

☐ Sack workers in the public sector.

☐ Raise food prices: reduce the distribution of subsidised food.

☐ Increase the price of services like public transport, electricity, public housing.

☐ Devalue the currency and therefore raise the cost of imports.

☐ Impose or raise charges for social services, such as education and health.

Whether or not these measures will prove effective is deeply debated. Few outside the IMF and the banking fraternity see how they can until the deeper problems of trade and raw material pric-

**THE COST OF DEBT, 1985**

| | Debt service as a percentage of National Income | Debt service as a percentage of Exports |
|---|---|---|
| KENYA | 6.9 | 25.5 |
| TANZANIA | 1.0 | 16.7 |
| PAKISTAN | 3.2 | 29.5 |
| BOLIVIA | 6.5 | 29.1 |
| EGYPT | 7.8 | 30.9 |
| JAMAICA | 23.5 | 36.5 |
| COSTA RICA | 13.3 | 36.6 |
| BRAZIL | 3.7 | 26.5 |
| MEXICO | 6.5 | 37.0 |
| ARGENTINA | 6.1 | 41.8 |
| (SUB SAHARAN AFRICA) | 4.8 | 21.5 |

ing have been addressed. In the meantime, the resources required to service the debt—that is, pay the interest and repay a proportion of the capital—continue to pour out of the countries who can spare them least. There is no sadder commentary on our inability to live the values of covenant and kingdom than that, in 1985, Africa paid more to service her debts than she received in famine-relief.

## 5. Technology

It may seem odd to include technology—or more precisely the transfer of inappropriate western technologies—as a major cause of the poverty of the Third World in general and the poorest among them in particular.

But we have already encountered a number of examples of exactly that. Medical technology is a case in point. The Philippines had, under President Marcos, the most modern cardiac hospital in Asia—and the worst provision of primary health care. The teaching hospital in Cote d'Ivoire consumed 80 per cent of the entire health budget. The state of the rest of the facilities can readily be imagined. Even in socialist Tanzania, where there has been the

## THE HUMAN COST OF DEBT

Zambia is a classic example of the problems of a country that relies on one export—copper—which the industrialised countries have been buying more and more cheaply. In order to go on importing goods and services, Zambia borrowed in the 1970s. But the 1980s saw the imposition of harsh 'conditions' by the International Monetary Fund. These had a direct effect on the urban poor: an effect reflected in the increase in the number of children dying from malnutrition and related diseases.

## RISE OF HUNGER

Protein Energy Malnutrition as a % of total hospital admissions and deaths

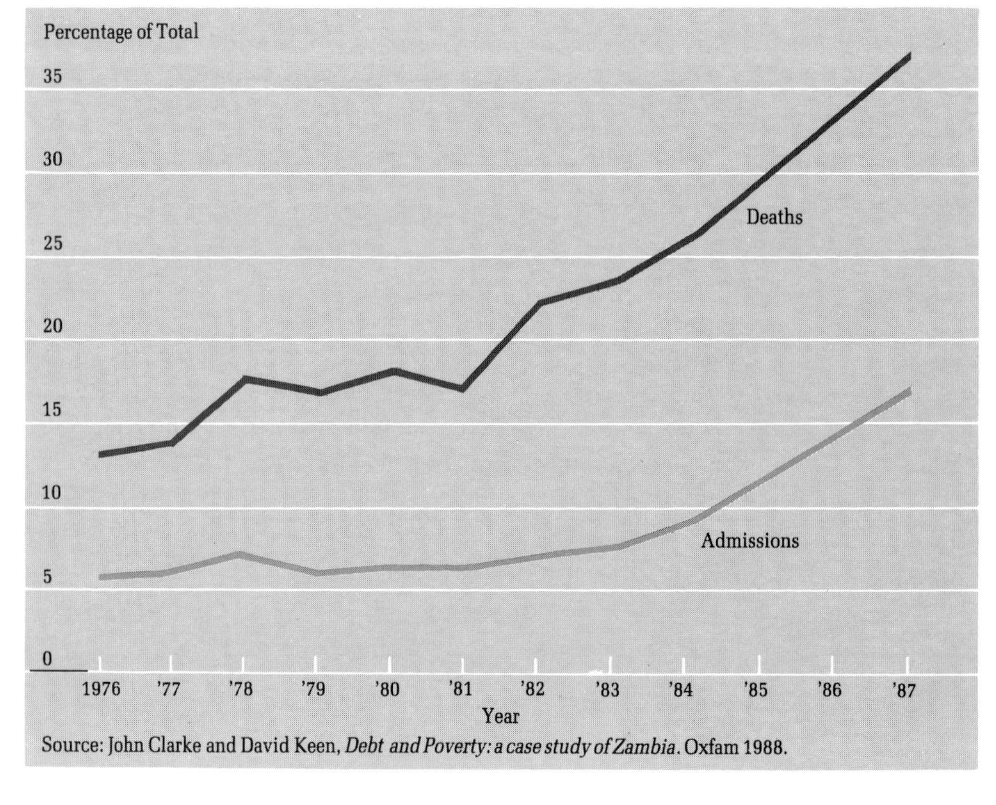


Source: John Clarke and David Keen, *Debt and Poverty: a case study of Zambia*. Oxfam 1988.

longest official interest in primary health care, it has in fact proved politically and professionally impossible to shift resources away from relatively high tech curative facilities towards low tech preventative and primary care.

There is something richly symbolic about high tech medicine. It is glamorous, mysterious, powerful, modern, impersonal and, allegedly, supremely scientific. Because it offers deliverance not only from sickness, but also from the mundane, the blatant, the ineffectual, the old fashioned and the obtrusively personal, it is bewitchingly attractive.

It is this transposition in cultural values that makes modern technology, in fields as diverse as road construction and crop protection, an easy sell in the Third World. But there are, of course, more down to earth reasons for its popularity.

First, it can be—indeed usually must be—bought with aid money. Because aid is tied to purchases from the donor country or is used directly to subsidise a commercial contract with a firm from the donor country, a project funded by aid monies is likely to incorporate the prevailing technology from the donor country. That will be, by the standards of the recipient country, 'high' tech.

Second, a foreign firm investing in a Third World country is likely to use the technology it knows best. While it may adjust it at the fringes (for instance using muscles rather than machines to move materials about), the core processes will be 'best practice' at home.

Third, consultants brought in to study a specific problem are likely to advise a technology that they are familiar with. The well-known American consulting firm, Arthur D. Little, for example, was asked to look at the distribution of meat in Brazil. It recommended a nation-wide 'Cold Chain Food System', which would oblige every slaughterhouse and food wholesaler to put in expensive and hard-to-maintain refrigerators, on the grounds, inter alia, that Brazil should prepare for a take-off in demand for 'TV dinners or other *important* frozen food items'.

The effects of this hard sell of high tech are little short of disasterous. They can be summarised thus:

□ A lot of the equipment breaks down quickly. There are no spares; no money to buy spares, and no one to fit them.

□ Most high tech displaces labour; compare a wheelbarrow with a bulldozer. Yet what people want most desperately is jobs.

□ It is often difficult to integrate one bit of high tech with other bits of low tech, for instance in a cotton mill. So there tends to be a knock-on effect that spreads high tech even though it is inappropriate.

□ High tech can seldom be copied locally. If you want more of it, you have to go abroad to buy it.

I shall have more to say about technology in Chapter 5. For the moment, the central point is that its export to other cultures is not only inappropriate and often misguided: it actually maintains people in poverty by consuming scarce resources that could be used more constructively and, most critically, depriving them of jobs.

**6. Tourism**

Although I shall have little to say about this, I want to mention it as a special case of the cultural impact of the rich world on the poor.

There is, of course, a wide spectrum of tourism, from the sensitive visitor who wants to learn as much as she can and stay as close to the local people as she can, to the barely disguised sex tourism that has become the scourge of some South East Asian and West African countries.

I am more concerned with the general case: that is with the average tourist who may well be full of good will and only wants to have a good holiday in the sun. What can be the harm in that?

The central question is what is known in the literature as the transfer of tastes. The consumption styles of tourists are inevitably catching. White bread made from imported wheat becomes fashionable. Imported foods and drinks slowly displace the locally produced varieties. Air conditioning becomes the mark of the man on his way up. Levis, Adidas, Coca Cola, Cannon, Kodak, Sony and Hitachi become the new gods of the elite—and then of the not-quite-so elite. Soon only the foreign is good enough; the local is inferior by definition, the second best that no one wants if it can be avoided. So in Trinidad lettuce is flown in from Florida—for local consumption.

It is no surprise to find the Premier of another Caribbean island reacting against the impact of tourism, not just on the economy of his island but on the dignity of his people:

> ...you will pardon me, I hope, if I appear not too anxious to grab the easiest dollar. The tourist dollar alone, unrestricted, is not worth the devastation of my people. A country where the people have lost their soul is no longer a country—and not worth visiting.

## PRAYER

The start of the prayer is to go back to the work you did on reflection on the love of God, and see it through the perspectives that have come alive for you in the analysis. Lay the one alongside the other, the reflection alongside the analysis. What strikes you as you do that?

This is not a quick or easy exercise. You may well find that it takes far longer than it has taken you to read thus far. Try not to hurry it. Give it all the time it needs. For God can disclose something of himself out of the work you have done if you give him time and space.

One of the things that you might ask him to disclose is where he is at work in all this. Pray to be given the grace to discern the kairos, the time of opportunity that is also the time of judgment, as God calls his creation forward into new relationships of mutuality and harmony. If we are in the time of creative change, where are changes necessary—and how may they be brought about? What, in a word, is God's agenda and what part are we being enabled to play in it?

Without generating an excessive sense of guilt, ask to be shown the places in your life where the values that maintain the structures of injustice have managed to establish themselves. You may find that this is a good time to look at questions of lifestyle, of economic priorities, of disciplined giving, of career ambitions. Quite other things might come up. Again, time and space—and the utter certainty of God's love for you just as you are—become central.

A final word of warning. We are called to live out the kingdom of God, to live its hopes and its values in all the choices we make. From that it does not follow that we are called to spread our energies thinly over every area where God is at work in his world. He is omnipotent and omniscient. We are neither! It takes time, discipline and discernment to know the area we are best suited to for both prayer and action. For some it will be peace; for others justice;

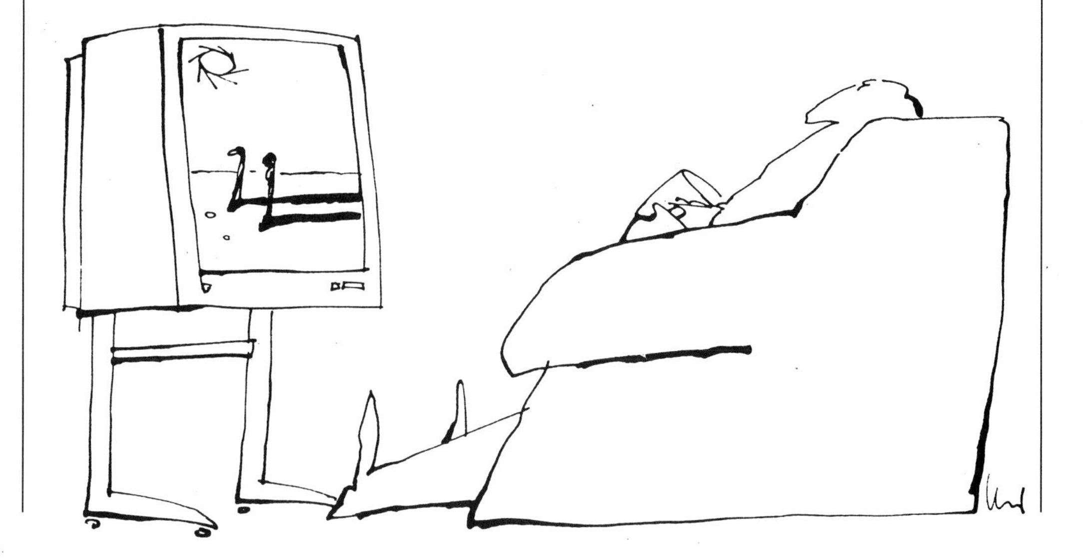

for others more focused parts of one of those subjects; for others something quite different. What is important is that we find what is right for us—and then resist the temptation to believe that the grass is greener or the going easier in some one else's patch. It seldom is.

If you think this may be 'your' area of involvement, here are some ideas—no more than random pointers—to where you might go from here.

## ACTION

So what can I do?

As I have already explained, there is no single answer to that. In the end we each have to take responsibility for our own decisions about where we think we are being led, and for working out the prayer and reflection which form the central element in the spirituality of action.

All I can do is offer a number of suggestions. I have grouped them for convenience into six sub-heads.

### 1. PRAYER AND THE CHURCH

Establish a discipline of prayer, either alone or in a group, to pray that our whole society may be delivered from the corporate greed and selfishness that makes the maintenance of unjust structures in trade and finance possible. Find out when there are major meetings of the IMF, the World Bank, Finance Ministers, UNCTAD and the GATT and make them the centre of your prayer.

Look carefully at the liturgy of your church. Where does it reflect these concerns—in thanksgiving, in confession and in intercession? Can you build a consensus in the church that they be incorporated regularly—without making them guilt-inducing?

Are these concerns included in the teaching ministry in your church? Can they be? (And it doesn't have to be the minister who does the teaching!)

Are they ever debated in the formal structures of your church? Would there be any point if they were? If you think there would, can you find a way of ensuring that they are?

### 2. DOING YOUR OWN ANALYSIS

How far is your bank involved in the debt issue? Are there any that are less involved? Why not ask to meet your regional director and ask him what steps the bank is taking to reduce the burden of debt, especially on the poorest countries?

What are the connections with the Third World of your community—its firms and businesses; its colleges and universities; its charities; private individuals who are or have recently worked in the Third World; people who visit it as tourists? What about the community as consumer? How do you assess the total impact of your community on the Third World? What can be done to make it more positive?

## 3. COMMUNITY EDUCATION

Can you help schools, colleges, youth groups to adopt stimulating and well informed programmes that help young people understand the issues and see them as moral and spiritual challenges? What resources would these organisations need to bring the programmes alive—films, videos, people, activities ... Can you help provide them?

Can you introduce simulation games such as 'Star Power' to community groups? ('Star Power', a particularly effective simulation game, is a way of exploring how it feels to be poor and powerless; and rich and successful. It is available in the UK from *Christian Aid*, Films and Publications Department, Interchurch House, P.O. Box 100, London SE1 7RT.)

What about well established community groups such as Chambers of Commerce, Rotary, Round Table, Inner Wheel, RAOB, British Legion ... is there any way of involving them in learning more about the real issues (and not just thinking they have done their bit when they have had a collection)?

Usually difficult but very important, can you start a dialogue with key local figures in the trade unions? Perhaps they could be persuaded to look at the relations of local employers with the Third World; and to put forward motions for debate in the annual conferences of their own unions and of the TUC.

## 4. ORGANISATIONS TO JOIN—AS RESOURCES AND AS PARTNERS

The World Development Movement is the most significant of the campaigning groups. It will keep you informed about what is going on and invite you to join its campaigns on specific issues.

Traidcraft is an effective way of tackling the trade issues as far as one's own lifestyle is concerned. Does your church have a regular Traidcraft stall?

All the major charities—Oxfam, War on Want, Tearfund, Christian Aid, Save the Children, Action Aid—do good work, especially in disaster situations. Some, especially Oxfam, War on Want and increasingly Action Aid, have a campaigning/education arm and these complement WDM.

There are a number of smaller charities that have a specialist appeal. Green Deserts is concerned with replanting forests in badly eroded/denuded areas. Tools for Development recycles disused garden and household tools for use in the Third World.

### 5. MEDIA

Monitor the output of all media—TV, radio and local radio, newspapers and magazines, to see what images they present of the Third World and the poorest in particular. Are they stereotyped images of 'the helpless native' or are they more accurate representations of the reality in which people find themselves? When a particularly good treatment appears, write and congratulate its author/producer/contributor.

Encourage your local paper and radio station to carry well researched but popular news/backgrounders on the Third World.

When articles on tourism in the Third World appear in the glossies, write and raise some of the questions about the negative impact of luxury tourism in poor countries—and keep badgering until you get a hearing.

### 6. POLITICAL

Most politicians imagine they can buy off the 'aid lobby' by promising to spend a bit more on aid. That isn't what it's all about—but you will have a job getting that through to most politicians, whether in power or aspiring to be. But keep after them. And remember always to speak or write in your own words about issues that you really know about. Try to know more than the politician, and never let him or her think that you are 'just another one of the aid stage army'.

Try to make sure that local party meetings discuss Third World issues, especially ahead of a major international conference/negotiation. Again, know your stuff and don't be scared to say your piece.

## APPRAISAL

At this stage, it is important to review the whole process and not just the action in which you have been involved.

You will probably find that your biggest difficulty has been properly integrating the 'outer' processes, like action and learning, with the 'inner' processes of prayer and reflection. The former tends to drive the latter out; or the latter acquires its own momentum and relates increasingly marginally to the former.

It is, none the less, one of the paradoxical graces of God that when the 'action' seems to have ended in failure and hurt and betrayal, as it sometimes will, the prayer comes alive. It is when we know our weakness and disobedience that the central motifs of life, death and resurrection acquire the most vibrant meaning.

Sometimes. However, that does not come easily. 'The dark night' can be a terrible experience; and in many ways it is the more terrible if the whole group shares it simultaneously. The rediscovery of the love of God then becomes the most pressing priority.

How we achieve that, or, better, allow ourselves to be given it again, cannot be predicted. I end, however, with a word of comfort from someone who knew all this at first hand: St Teresa of Avila.

> Though we do not have our Lord with us in bodily presence, we have our neighbour, who, for the ends of love and loving service, is as good as our Lord himself.

Chapter Two

# THE ENVIRONMENT

## REFLECTION ON THE LOVE OF GOD

READ GENESIS 1:26–31 & 2:5–8

God said, 'Let us make man in our own image, in the likeness of ourselves, and let them be masters of the fish of the sea, the birds of heaven, the cattle, all the wild beasts and all the reptiles that crawl upon the earth'.

God created man in the image of himself,
in the image of God he created him,
male and female he created them.

God blessed them, saying to them, 'Be fruitful, multiply, fill the earth and conquer it. Be masters of the fish of the sea, the birds of heaven and all living animals on the earth.' God said, 'See, I give you all the seed-bearing plants that are upon the whole earth, and all the trees with seed-bearing fruit; this shall be your food. To all wild beasts, all birds of heaven and all living reptiles on the earth I give all the foliage of plants for food. And so it was. God saw all he had made, and indeed it was very good. Evening came and morning came: the sixth day ...

At the time when Yahweh God made earth and heaven there was as yet no wild bush on the earth nor had any wild plant yet sprung up, for Yahweh God had not sent rain on the earth, nor was there any man to till the soil. However, a flood was rising from the earth and watering all the surface of the soil. Yahweh God fashioned man of dust from the soil. Then he breathed into his nostrils a breath of life, and thus man became a living being.

Yahweh God planted a garden in Eden which is in the east, and there he put the man he had fashioned.

Here we have two creation myths, from two different sources, reflecting two different theological interests. The centre of interest in the first is the primacy of Yahweh, the creator and sustainer. The centre of the second is an exploration of the tragedy of the human condition. The origin of that tragedy is taken to be disobedience and arrogance.

From our standpoint, the interest lies in the very different accounts they give of the place of mankind in the created order, and more particularly the way mankind is seen as relating to the rest of the creation. In the first account, usually called the Priestly account, people are seen as being 'masters' of creation, destined to 'subdue' it. Nature, then, is subservient to their needs. It is the raw material out of which humankind will wrest a living.

By contrast, the second account has mankind as the caretaker of creation. Their role is, as it were, to bring creation to its finest expression. In both accounts, Yahweh's creative power is seen as an expression of his love—he gives, he blesses, he offers, he brings companionship, he displays his handiwork. If creation is an act of love, which perception of mankind's role in it is the more consistent: as master or as caretaker?

READ EXODUS 16:1–5

From Elim they set out again, and the whole community of the sons of Israel reached the wilderness of Sin—between Elim and Sinai—on the fifteenth day of the second month after they had left Egypt. And the whole community of the sons of Israel began to complain against Moses and Aaron in the wilderness and said to them, 'Why did we not die at Yahweh's hand in the land of Egypt, when we were able to sit down to pans of meat and could eat bread to our heart's content! As it is, you have brought us to this wilderness to starve this whole company to death!'

Then Yahweh said to Moses, 'Now I will rain down bread for you from the heavens. Each day the people are to go out and gather the day's portion; I propose to test them in this way to see whether they will follow my law or not. On the sixth day, when they prepare what they have brought in, this will be twice as much as the daily gathering.'

The story of Exodus is often seen as the story of deliverance from slavery in Egypt to settlement in a land flowing with milk and honey. It is also, however, the story of Israel's experience of the terror of an infertile land, a land in which nothing will grow, in which no wild animals can survive, in which famine and drought are the only constants.

Here Israel is brought face to face with two fundamental facts of its life: that the promise of land alone, of land apart from the covenant-love of Yahweh, is useless; and that they can indeed rely on the love of Yahweh as long as they are faithful to their side of the covenant relationship.

READ PSALM 8

Yahweh, our Lord,
how great your name throughout the earth!

Above the heavens is your majesty chanted
by the mouths of children, babes in arms.
You set your stronghold firm against your foes
to subdue enemies and rebels.

I look up at your heavens, made by your fingers,
at the moon and stars you set in place—
ah, what is man that you should spare a thought for him,
the son of man that you should care for him?

Yet you have made him little less than a god,
you have crowned him with glory and splendour,
made him lord over the work of your hands,
set all things under his feet,

sheep and oxen, all these,
yes, wild animals too,

birds in the air, fish in the sea
travelling the paths of the ocean.

Yahweh, our Lord,
how great your name throughout the earth!

We seem to be back with the first of the Genesis accounts of mankind's relationship to the natural order. Mankind has been made 'Lord'. It is of course entirely possible to read the text in that way—and it is probable that the writer thought of man as lord of all creation in the most obvious sense. The Jewish-Christian heritage is open to the charge of encouraging that strain of thought.

We may, however, do well to remember both contemporary Jewish and later Christian ideas of 'lordship'. David's son Solomon, from whose time this Psalm might originate, had developed a new approach to kingship. His central aim, so his historians tell us, was to acquire and share with his people 'wisdom', a sense that is of the interconnectedness and wholeness of all human affairs.

Christians saw Jesus as taking that further. His interpretation of 'lordship' meant assuming the role of the born slave, the lowliest person in the household. Seen in those terms, the Lord of creation becomes the humble caretaker.

READ LUKE 8:4–15

With a large crowd gathering and people from every town finding their way to him, he used this parable:

'A sower went out to sow his seed. As he sowed, some fell on the edge of the path and was trampled on; and the birds of the air ate it up. Some seed fell on rock, and when it came up it withered away, having no moisture. Some seed fell amongst thorns and the thorns grew with it and choked it. And some seed fell into rich soil and grew and produced its crop a hundredfold.' Saying this he cried, 'Listen, anyone who has ears to hear!'

His disciples asked him what this parable might mean, and he said, 'The mysteries of the kingdom of God are revealed to you; for the rest there are only parables, so that

they may see but not perceive,
listen but not understand.

'This, then, is what the parable means: the seed is the word of God. Those on the edge of the path are people who have heard it, and then the devil comes and carries away the word from their hearts in case they should believe and be saved. Those on the rock are people who, when they first hear it, welcome the word with joy. But these have no root; they believe for a while, and in time of trial they give up. As for the part that fell into thorns, this is people who have heard, but as they go on their way they are choked by the worries and riches and pleasures of life and do not reach maturity. As for the part in the rich soil, this is people with a noble and generous heart who have heard the word and take it to themselves and yield a harvest through their perseverance.'

Many of Jesus' parables draw heavily from a close observation of nature. Like most of his contemporaries, especially those of the artisan class, Jesus lived near enough nature to let it form his thought and speech patterns. But this story is interesting for two reasons.

First, it shows that Jesus was not a dreamy romantic about the processes of nature. Pests, disease, drought and bad husbandry are facts of life; part of the human condition that orthodox Jews of his day would explain in terms of the sin of Adam and Eve. We may prefer a slightly more careful language, but Christians recognise that human beings and the whole natural order 'has fallen' from what God intended and intends it to be.

Second, Jesus constantly draws parallels between the life of nature and the inner life of men and women. However much 'master of the world' humankind may be, we are not apart from nature. We share not only the physical laws of nature, but at a much deeper level, the way we grow—or wither—in the spiritual life reflects what is going on around us in the natural environment.

READ ROMANS 8:18–25

I think that what we suffer in this life can never be compared to the glory, as yet unrevealed, which is waiting for us. The whole creation is eagerly waiting for God to reveal his sons. It was not for any fault on the part of creation that it was made unable to attain its purpose, it was made so by God; but creation still retains the hope of being freed, like us, from its slavery to decadence, to enjoy the same freedom and glory as the children of God. From the beginning till now the entire creation, as we know, has been groaning in one great act of giving birth; and not only creation, but all of us who possess the first-fruits of the Spirit, we too groan inwardly as we wait for our bodies to be set free. For we must be content to hope that we shall be saved—our salvation is not in sight, we should not have to be hoping for it if it were— but, as I say, we must hope to be saved since we are not saved yet—it is something we must wait for with patience.

The key verse is 22. It is a magnificent vision of the whole of creation, to be thought of as including but going far beyond the natural environment to embrace, for instance, generations past and generations as yet unborn. This whole creation, Paul says, is waiting for its final liberation. It is groaning in the act of labour, struggling to realise the glory for which it was made and to which it will be drawn by the love of God.

In this vision, then, creation is not something that has reached its apogee already and is now, as it were, slowly winding down. Rather, it is waiting to be set free from the inner destructiveness that prevents it adequately reflecting the joy and harmony of its Creator. And this period of waiting is full of tension, anxiety, pain and struggle. The future is promised—but it is still not realised.

READ PHILIPPIANS 2:1–11

If our life in Christ means anything to you, if love can persuade at all, or the Spirit that we have in common, or any tenderness and sympathy, then be united in your convictions and united in your love, with a common purpose and a common mind. That is the one thing which would make me completely happy. There must be no competition among you, no conceit; but everybody is to be self-effacing. Always consider the other person to be better than yourself, so that nobody thinks of his own interests first but

everybody thinks of other people's
interests instead. In your minds you
must be the same as Christ Jesus:

His state was divine,
yet he did not cling
to his equality with God
but emptied himself
to assume the condition of a slave,
and became as men are;
and being as all men are,
he was humbler yet,
even to accepting death,
death on a cross.
But God raised him high
and gave him the name
which is above all other names
so that *all beings*
in the heavens, on earth and in the underworld,
*should bend the knee* at the name of Jesus
and that every tongue should acclaim
Jesus Christ as Lord,
to the glory of God the Father.

This reading brings together the themes we have begun to explore in Psalm 8 and in Romans 8. Two thoughts, both central to the Christian faith, lie side by side. The first puts the virtue of gentleness at the heart of the Christian character. Christ expresses that gentleness most completely when he 'empties himself' by becoming man. He lays aside all claim to authority, to power, to control and becomes the recipient of other people's authority. That leads him to the cross.

But the cross is the origin of the final redemption of the whole cosmos. Verse 10 alludes to the three orders of creation, 'all the living things', and sees them as redeemed to worship Christ as Lord. By using a formula found in Isaiah 45:23 the author of this hymn or poem (who may or may not have been Paul himself) identifies Christ with the creative power and love of Yahweh. As one, they bring together the final redemption of the whole created order.

As you let these passages settle in your mind and heart, you might like to bear the following questions in mind:

☐ To which model of mankind's relationship to nature does our society and culture cling: that of master or that of caretaker?

☐ What difference to the choice of that model does Christ's life, death and resurrection make?

☐ What sense can we make of the notion of the whole of creation waiting, groaning, being in labour?

These readings point very clearly to the cross and resurrection as *the* kairos, the turning point of the inner history of humankind. What do they have to say about the role we are called to play in the kairos of our days?

It would be a pity if these questions became a kind of school exam! They are intended less to challenge your intellectual powers than to be points of reference to which you will want to return as the cycle progresses, and to be themes that help you digest the readings. That digestion is important. For without digestion the material can never provide nourishment for the journey ahead.

## ANALYSIS

Once a human body loses a third of its skin the life of the patient is at very serious risk. Once a tree loses a third of its bark, it is likely to die. Many ecologists now argue that once the planet loses a third of its forests, its survival is at risk. The planet earth has already lost 32 per cent of its forests. The loss of the next 1 per cent may be profitable to the individual logging company or a host of individual families who clear the forest to grow their food, but to the planet as a whole ... ?

This illustration raises two related issues with which we shall be concerned throughout this section: the interconnectedness of the ecosystem, and the way in which men and women use, misuse and abuse their role in that interconnectedness. We must start by having a closer look at this interdependence.

In a healthy ecosystem, the parts relate to each other in a way that keeps the whole system functioning. The health of each part both depends upon and helps determine the health of the whole system. For example, in moist tropical forest, the litter on the forest floor is broken down by insects and fungi. The cellulose of the original litter is transformed into nutrients which are re-absorbed by the trees. Formed into wood or leaves, they are eventually returned to the forest floor. Within that plant system, there are many subsystems: birds predate upon insects which predate upon other insects which feed on the leaves of plants.

Environmental stress occurs when one part of the ecosystem can no longer fulfil its role with respect to other parts of the system. Now some stress is endemic in the environment: indeed a stressless ecosystem is quite rare. For example, a hard winter in northern Europe will kill a high proportion of many forms of plant and animal life. It will take time for the system to readjust and in the process other forms of stress may appear.

Suppose, however, that the plants involved in this illustration do not recover. Then the system cannot return to 'normal'. A new equilibrium or point of balance will have to be found and that process may itself involve very far-reaching changes, not only to the bird population, but to plants, insects, and even possibly mammals. If the initial disturbance is sufficiently large, whole species may disappear in an area, and if the initial disturbance occurs in all the habitats of the species, then the species may disappear altogether.

Stress, then, is itself a 'natural' condition of the environment. The equilibrium is always moving. Indeed Darwinians would argue that it is itself a stimulus to adaptation, change and survival.

The difficulties arise when the scale, frequency and range of stress to which the ecosystem is subject becomes so great that return to equilibrium in any recognisable sense becomes impossible.

When people talk today of an environmental crisis, they are haunted by the fear that the level of stress has reached a point from which there is no return. In every case, it is man's impact on the environment that is producing that stress. It is to some examples of man-made stress that we must now turn.

We begin with population, not necessarily because it is quantitively the most important factor, but because it is the one which tends to be given the most prominence. That itself is revealing: because 'the population problem' is thought to be someone else's—namely the Third World's—affair, we are quick to emphasise it, readily forgetting that it is not only the *numbers* of people that pose the problem; but also the *demands* those people make on the environment. I shall argue later that levels of consumption and forms of economic organisation are much more of a threat to the environment than population numbers alone.

## POPULATION PRESSURE

The carrying capacity of an ecosystem under a given level of technology is limited. If more and more is expected of it, without changing the way the ecosystem works (for example, by introducing irrigation), it begins to show signs of stress and will finally break down.

The classic example of this happening is to be found in Africa, in parts of Asia and in much of Central and South America. At the centre of ecological stress and breakdown there is the effect of shortening fallow cycles on slash and burn agriculture. In conditions of low population density, slash and burn is an efficient way for poor people with simple technology to get a high output per hour of labour. Diagram 1 shows the system operating in such a context.

The cultivating family operates in square 1 for two or three years. Branches are lopped off trees, some trees are felled and, in the ash gardens that result from the burning of this timber, crops are grown. Good yields are achieved.

By the end of the second or third year readily accessible timber

## SLASH AND BURN

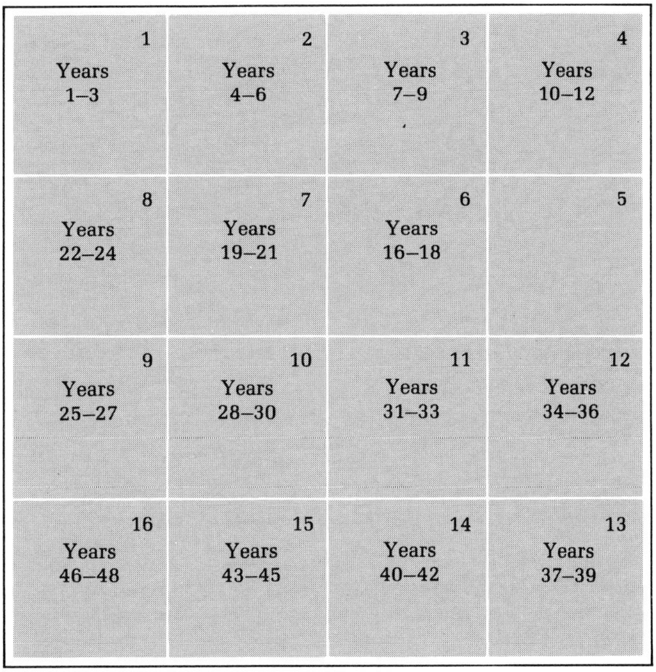

Diagram 1

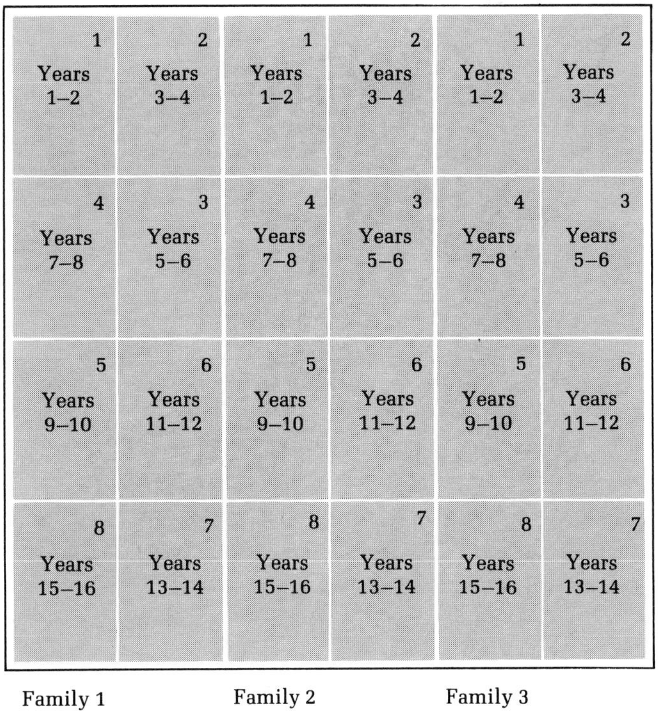

| | | | |
|---|---|---|---|
| 1 Years 1–3 | 2 Years 4–6 | 3 Years 7–9 | 4 Years 10–12 |
| 8 Years 22–24 | 7 Years 19–21 | 6 Years 16–18 | 5 |
| 9 Years 25–27 | 10 Years 28–30 | 11 Years 31–33 | 12 Years 34–36 |
| 16 Years 46–48 | 15 Years 43–45 | 14 Years 40–42 | 13 Years 37–39 |

Diagram 2

| Family 1 | | Family 2 | | Family 3 | |
|---|---|---|---|---|---|
| 1 Years 1–2 | 2 Years 3–4 | 1 Years 1–2 | 2 Years 3–4 | 1 Years 1–2 | 2 Years 3–4 |
| 4 Years 7–8 | 3 Years 5–6 | 4 Years 7–8 | 3 Years 5–6 | 4 Years 7–8 | 3 Years 5–6 |
| 5 Years 9–10 | 6 Years 11–12 | 5 Years 9–10 | 6 Years 11–12 | 5 Years 9–10 | 6 Years 11–12 |
| 8 Years 15–16 | 7 Years 13–14 | 8 Years 15–16 | 7 Years 13–14 | 8 Years 15–16 | 7 Years 13–14 |

is becoming scarce and the original ash garden is exhausted, not least because heavy tropical rain is likely to have leached out many of the nutrients from the soil. It is therefore time to move on to square 2, and so the whole family migrates a mile or two and the process is repeated in square 2.

We may assume the family moves across the grid in the first diagram until it has reached square 16. If we assume three years per square, forty-five years will have passed since it left square 1. In that period secondary bush will have re-established itself. The lopped trees will have re-grown and the bush will have recovered. It can therefore withstand the return of the family and the repetition of the process.

Suppose, however, that a second and third family appears on this grid and assume that the three families agree to split the grid in three, but continue the process otherwise unchanged, as in the second diagram. Now the cycle will take only fifteen years instead of forty-eight, and when our original family returns to square 1, it will find that the bush has not fully recovered.

It will therefore have to be much more vigorous in its cutting of the bush in order to collect enough timber to create an ash garden. That in turn means that when the family comes back to square 1 for

A Malaysian farmer burns bamboo to clear his land and make it more fertile. If accompanied by population pressure, this 'slash and burn' method can have disastrous long-term consequences for farmland.

a third time it will find the process of recovery even less far advanced.

The impact is far reaching. For in their search for wood the family has now, we may assume, destroyed the tree cover and exposed the weak lateritic soils to their two worst enemies—heavy tropical rain and hot, unfiltered sun. The rain washes the soil away and the sun bakes what is left into a hard, infertile crust. Erosion, and in extreme cases desertification, are now inevitable.

The natural environment is destroyed, but so, too, is our family. They can no longer make ash gardens because there is no wood to produce the ash. The soil has become quite infertile: indeed most of it has been washed away. The family has neither tools nor technology to practise any other kind of farming. Failing outside help or migration to an area under less pressure (which is becoming increasingly hard to find in many developing countries), they will simply starve to death.

This highly schematic account describes the process of land degradation that follows population pressure that is now common in many parts of Africa—from North and Central Ethiopia throughout the Sahel, East and Central Africa to the so-called Homelands of South Africa. It can be found, too, in most Asian countries and,

Almost one-third of land on earth is desert—and the deserts are steadily growing. 80 million people, in nearly 100 countries, are directly threatened by desertification. This village, in Western Sudan, is on the front line.

with variations, in practically every country of Latin America.

In some of these countries, for example, Zaire, Brazil, Zambia, there is still land available for those prepared to move from over-populated areas to under-populated areas. This very fact can make people resistant to taking simple conservation measures. In 1986 I was in Southern Tanzania pleading with a group of peasant farmers to keep their cattle out of a gully which was beginning to erode severely. The head man of the village shrugged his shoulders and smiled: 'Don't worry, bwana. When this place is no good, we will move over there'—and he waved in the direction of some low undulating hills where we both knew there was indeed plenty of land.

Moving is not always easy. It involves moving from one ethnic and language group to another which may not be welcoming. It is thus no surprise to find that when governments have sponsored large-scale movements of people from over-populated into under-populated areas that there is a steady trickle (and sometimes even a flood) of returnees who prefer the harsh and unpromising life that they know to abundant land in an area surrounded by actual or potential enemies far removed from their own kinsmen. The Bangladeshi government's attempts to settle people from the overcrowded delta in the Chittagong hills is one, blood-stained, example.

The mechanism of environmental breakdown I have described is based on one form of agriculture. Environmental degradation can also result from two agricultural systems coming into conflict. In the Saharan fringes of West Africa, for example, the agricultural system best suited to the unreliable rainfall and light soils is that of pastoralism—that is, mobile herders who can move their flocks to wherever there is grazing and water. Typically, these herders move into the interior during the rains, to take advantage of the short flush of grass in the brief rainy period, and then move back towards the heavier rainfall areas in the south as the grass is burnt up in the desert fringes.

As long as the herdsmen can move uninhibited to fresh grazing, this is an efficient system of land use, albeit with a very low carrying capacity. In many sub-Sahelian states, such as Ghana, Upper Volta and the Ivory Coast, population growth has meant that people have been pushed further north to the forest fringes and into the Savannah areas, and have established themselves there as cultivators. These lands have thus become closed to the herdsmen who have traditionally sought refuge in them. They are caught between a desert that cannot sustain them and the farms of the new settlers that will not admit them. All they can do is sell their cattle

Increasing herd sizes and dwindling pastures lead to over-grazing, which exhausts the land. These herds are grazing in Sudan.

at catastrophically low prices and buy grain produced on the newly settled arable land while they wait for the rains to return.

This series of events shows the environment under stress, but not irrecoverably so. There is a variant of this scenario, however, that has a more long-lasting effect on the environment. If the herdsmen are unable to sell their cattle and manage to eke out an existence around a well sunk by the government or an aid agency, the stock will survive—but the range will not. Grazed to disappearing point and trampled unceasingly, it will be killed, to be replaced by harsh, inedible plants adapted to so hostile an environment. Once such plants have established themselves, they will drive out the more nutritious grasses.

Next time the herds return, they find the environment will not sustain them. In schematic form, this is the root cause of the Sahelian droughts and famines in 1973 and 1983.

A further variation on the same theme, this time from Asia, is worth recording for two reasons: it demonstrates the way in which the natural environment operates as a system, and it shows how one episode of stress can have far-reaching effects a great distance away.

Bangladesh is a country of 100 million people. The vast majority live on the Ganges delta. They are therefore at the end of one of the greatest rivers of the world, which rises in Nepal and passes through Northern India. Traditionally, the delta of the Ganges has been fertile as a result of the annual flooding of the river and the deposit of fertile silts on the flood plain.

In recent years, however, two things have changed. First, the settlement of the steep slopes of the head-waters of many of the tributaries of the Ganges, primarily in Nepal, have greatly increased the volume of soil washed down by the river in the rainy season.

It might be thought that this would be welcome in Bangladesh, even though it clearly poses a long-term problem for those whose land is thus being eroded. The reality however is different. The slow-moving waters of the Ganges delta allow much of this material to sink to the bottom of the river, thus raising the level of the river. With its carrying capacity thus reduced, the river generates a greater volume of flooding over a wider area. The flood tragedy of 1987 is the direct result.

Furthermore, with a rapidly growing and already densely settled population, Bangladesh needs to improve its agriculture. More particularly, it needs to adopt the techniques of the so-called Green Revolution. Central to these techniques is control of the irrigation water. With much of its territory flooded for three to four months of the year, Bangladesh is unable to adopt the agricultural techniques which would enable it to feed itself. With the river beds increasingly congested, the cost of flood control is far beyond the capacity of Bangladesh, even with substantial support from the major aid donors.

Environmental stress in Nepal, directly related to the growing population there, thus puts at risk the lives and livelihoods of the people of Bangladesh. A formerly beneficent cycle of fertilisation and flooding of the Ganges Delta has become, as a result of increased population at both ends of that river, a vicious cycle that leaves most observers of Bangladesh fearful of more serious floods and of a major famine in that country before the end of the century.

These three examples are enough to establish the point. Population pressure unattended by technical change to reduce the demands of traditional systems upon the environment is leading to environmental stress on a scale that has, within the last fifteen years, cost certainly millions and on some reckonings tens of millions of lives. Although some of those lives were lost in the well-publicised famines of 1973 and 1983, many more are lost year in and year out by the less dramatic collapse of living standards among peoples facing the consequences of environmental degradation. For the collapse of living standards brings in its train lower

Pollution is sometimes in the eye of the beholder. Refineries are notorious polluters. Poppies may look fair enough, but if they make marijuana...?

We hardly find pollution in our own industrial heartlands shocking any more...but when one of the noblest buildings in the world is threatened...?

planes of nutrition, higher infant mortality, lower life expectancy.

For all their horror for the people caught in an environmental breakdown—and the pictures that came out of Ethiopia in 1983-5 and again in 1987-8 brought home the dimensions of that horror—the environmental stress and breakdown that I have been describing thus far has an innocence about it that heightens both its tragedy and its despair. The people of Bangladesh have committed no sin, no act of hubris. The famine victims in the Sahel and Ethiopia have done as their ancestors have done. They have been faithful to their ancient wisdoms. Their only crime has been to fail to detect the inflexibility of those wisdoms in the face of gently, inexorably, rising numbers: or, having half-detected it, to fail to fashion an adequate response.

That is their tragedy and their despair. Within the means available to them, there is no adequate response. They become dependent upon the means of others: governments, aid agencies, voluntary workers, crisis managers. Lacking adequate understanding of both people and ecosystem, lacking resources, time and commitment, these latter cannot be judged harshly if their solutions too often turn out to be inadequate in scale, conception and duration—in a word, half-baked. The truth is that we do not know how to handle large scale ecological breakdown. Perhaps we would do less damage if we started by acknowledging at least that much.

When we turn from environmental stress that stems from growing numbers to stress that stems from greed, we lose the innocence but gain little wisdom. There seems a juggernaut effect at work that makes reversal of our sources of environmental stress so slow that it may be too late. There are many reasons for that: some are technical; but many more are ethical. Unlike the Tuareg in the Sahel or the Bengalis in the Ganges Delta or the Nepalis in the Himalayan foothills, we have choices to make. We do not lack for alternatives: *our* tragedy is that we lack the wisdom to make them. Perhaps they will yet be forced upon us.

## ENVIRONMENTAL STRESS IN THE NORTH ATLANTIC COMMUNITIES

But that is to anticipate a discussion to which we shall have to return. It is time now to do for our culture—that of the rich North Atlantic communities—what we have done for the poor communities of the South: examine some of the areas of environmental stress.

It is dangerous, however, to over-draw that contrast. As a preface to a discussion of air pollution in Europe, let me confess that it came as a surprise to me to discover, for example, that the greatest threat to the Taj Mahal, the epitome of romantic creativity, lies in the sulphurous emissions of the thousands of smoke stacks of small industries in the Agra area. The Indian government is now so alarmed at the actual and potential damage to the Taj Mahal from atmospheric pollution that, despite its desperate need to provide employment for its urban population, it is taking steps to close down and/or relocate many of the industries in the Agra region.

That is only the most poignant example. In many Third World cities, atmospheric pollution has already reached levels that threaten not only the health and well-being of the urban population, but the very survival of ecosystems down-wind of the cities themselves. If in what follows we concentrate on Western Europe and North America, then, it should not be assumed that the phenomenon we describe is related only to the most highly industrialised areas.

## Acid rain

Acid rain and its associated pollutants know no boundaries. Almost by definition, in Europe at least, acid rain falls on countries other than those that generate it, since it takes time for the pollutants to rise in the atmosphere, be absorbed in rain clouds and then be dropped as rain with high acidity levels. As the air is moving during this process, the acid rain is carried far from the source of the pollution.

The effects are both bizarre and unjust. All but a few countries export to other countries at least half of the sulphur dioxide they emit. The most successful exporter is the United Kingdom. The largest emitter of sulphur in Europe, it exports nearly two thirds of that sulphur almost entirely to northern Europe. By contrast, Austria which emits only one tenth as much sulphur as the United Kingdom, none the less suffers more depositions of sulphur per hectare than the UK.

Sulphur levels in the atmosphere, resulting largely from the burning of fossil fuel and the smelting of metallic ores, have begun to decline in both the US and Europe, but there is still more than twice as much sulphur in the world's atmosphere as there was in 1950.

The *scale* involved is hard to grasp. For example, one large North American nickel smelter annually releases more than twice as much sulphur as was released by the eruption of the volcano at Mount St Helens in May, 1980.

It is not only sulphur, however, that causes problems. Although the chemistry is often complex, sulphur and nitrogen oxides combine with other pollutants in the atmosphere and with harmless minerals in the earth to produce deadly cocktails. For example, one reason for what is known in Germany as *Waldsterben* (literally forest-death) is the effect that acid rain (mostly sulphur) has on heavy metals in the soil. These are dissolved by the acid rain and recombine with chemical elements in the acid rain to become highly toxic. Trees are thus poisoned through the root system.

No wonder scientists in New Jersey studying threats to pine forests concluded that of drought, fire, insects, pests and ozone, acid rain has emerged as 'the most widespread, long-lasting and severe in its effects on the trees' growth histories'.

The trouble does not end, however, with the destruction of trees. Acid rain and heavy metals act on mosses, algae, nitrogen fixing bacteria and fungi, and thus greatly reduce the natural fertility of the litter on the forest floors. In extreme cases, as reported in both Germany and Austria, the forest floor can become so infertile that not only is natural forest regeneration impossible, but replanting with young trees is ineffective. The whole ecosystem has been destroyed. The land is useless.

A misreading of the creation mandate to 'subdue the earth' has frequently led western cultures to exploit nature and humanity whatever the cost. This view of 19th century Bradford, England, was typical of the Industrial Revolution.

Unfortunately it is difficult to give precise estimates of the scale of the problem of acid rain. That is partly because acid rain itself is a rather imprecise term and partly because the scale of damage directly attributable to acid rain and its associated pollutants varies from year to year. Sometimes acid rain comes as the last straw to a forest environment already under stress from drought or frost or fire. None the less, some estimates are striking. In the summer of 1983 the German government reported the value of trees that had been lost as a result of acid rain at $1.2 billion. A few months later, a fourfold increase in forest damage was recorded. In Central Europe it is thought that between 3.5 and 4 million hectares—an area roughly half the size of Austria—have been damaged by pollutants. Environmental scientists in Poland and Czechoslovakia have warned that if the nations of Central Europe increase the use of high sulphur coal over the next few years as currently planned, then a further 3 million hectares of forest will be damaged, perhaps irreversibly.

The wider ramifications of atmospheric pollution in terms of its long-run effect on other organisms than trees are still unclear. In the early seventies Lester Lane and Eugene Seskin synthesised research from all over the world and found a strong relationship between the level of air pollution and the incidence of respiratory disease. That does not necessarily establish a causal connection, but subsequent work has shown that high levels of air pollution, especially of lead, can increase the incidence of emphysema, stomach and lung cancer and coronary disease. There is strong evidence that lead poisoning from car exhaust fumes contributes to brain damage in children. In urban areas with heavy traffic patterns, the statistical incidence of brain damage is significantly higher than in rural areas.

Man, then, stews in his own polluted juices. What is less clear is the effect of air pollution on other mammals. Studies of foxes, various species of birds and of deer suggest that a range of diseases are associated with the toxic effects of air pollution—from abortion to an inability to digest food properly.

Can it be turned around? Can acid rain, for example, the basic causes of which are well known and fairly easily located, be prevented? Technically there is no difficulty in removing sulphur and nitrogen from smoke: but it *is* expensive. One estimate is that it can add 20 per cent to the basic cost of a power station. Even if that is on the high side (because, for example, it takes no account of economies of scale), the implied additional cost of producing power is much less (since in thermal stations the capital cost is substantially less than a third of the full cost of production). As a rough guide we could say that cleaning up thermal power stations might add 6–10 per cent to the cost of producing electricity: and only 2–5 per cent to electricity bills (since generating costs are about a third of consumers' costs).

Such sums can easily miss the point. As Schumacher reminded us, it was none other than Keynes who put economics in its proper perspective, admonishing us not to 'overstate the importance of the economic problem, or sacrifice to its supposed necessities other matters of greater and more permanent importance'. None the less, the evidence is that that is exactly what we—or at least some of us—are in the process of doing. While in a five year crash programme Germany plans to spend £9,800 million on fitting flue-desulphurisation plants to 80 per cent of her thermal stations, the British Central Electricity Generating Board intends to spend just £600 million on three of its forty-one thermal stations—and that over a ten year period. In that time some of the other (dirtier) stations will go out of service, but by the end of the century Britain's contribution to the atmospheric pollution of northern Europe will still be large enough to pose a major threat to the forests and lakes and perhaps health of her neighbours. It is no surprise that Greenpeace complained, in 1987, to the UK Advertising Standards Authority about CEGB advertising that claimed that the Board was 'mounting an extensive programme of counter measures'. Privately, Board officials admit that with privatisation plans under way for the industry, higher expenditures on 'non-productive' (i.e. non-profit-making) activities were unacceptable. That is a point to which we shall have to return.

It poses, though, a key issue: there is often a direct conflict between private profit and public environmental damage. Two examples will suffice. Many endangered species, from whales to turtles, are endangered only because someone can make a profit from destroying them. And those who do make a profit resist strenuously any attempt to control their activities. The blatant abuse of 'scientific' whaling concessions by the Japanese and the resistance of the French to the control of international trade in turtles suggested by the Convention of International Trade in Endangered Species are only two examples. They demonstrate that those who traffic in endangered species will do their best to get round whatever restrictions the international community can agree to impose. If governments resist overtly, traders continue covertly. Despite harsh penalties, the trade in rhino horns, a coveted aphrodisiac in Asia, is still alive and well—as corpses in the African bush (and game parks) and market stalls in Hong Kong and Shanghai attest.

## Farming and factories

The second example is less exotic—and in many ways much trickier. There is no doubt that farming technology in Europe and North America has had a major impact on the countryside. The list of practices that create stress for local ecosystems is as familiar as it is long: grubbing up hedges and orchards; spraying herbicides and pesticides; use of chemical fertilisers; monocropping; intensive management of grassland systems; deliberate eradication of pests, including foxes, badgers and moles; overstocking of commons and hills; careless management of wastes and slurries; ploughing up wetlands and other important or scarce habitats; single-species tree planting.

The debate about the precise environmental impact of these practices generates more heat than light, not least because *aesthetic* considerations tend to get confused with strictly ecological. That many species of fauna and flora have disappeared from vast areas of continents is true and sad—but it does not represent actual or potential damage equivalent to acid rain or deforestation. In most countries there are parks or other protected sites where the 'original' (itself a highly imprecise term) ecosystem survives. There may not be enough of them, they may be inadequately protected and ungenerously funded, but they act as both a museum and a stockhouse.

Those who take a more negative view of the ecological impact of 'high' farming—and who share my entirely negative view about its aesthetic impact—have to face a difficult question. In a highly competitive industry in which higher costs cannot be passed on in the form of higher prices, to what extent is it reasonable to expect the individual to forego income in order to provide a public service—the conservation of particular habitats or the preservation of visual amenities? The grain barons of East Anglia can no doubt 'afford' more than an over-mortgaged young hill farmer in Wales, but unfortunately there is no necessary concurrence between ecological desirability and financial strength.

I am suspicious of arguments that demand from one section of the community a more highly developed sense of the public good than from everyone else. If we want to preserve particular habitats and ecosystems—the Somerset Wetlands, the Norfolk Broads, the Yorkshire Wolds—the community as a whole has to take responsibility, including financial responsibility. That may mean subsidising a group of farmers to farm in a non-optimal way—for example, reducing the use of chemical fertiliser or grazing grasslands very lightly—or to plant specific crops, such as hardwoods. So far we have been loud in our condemnation of 'modern farming', but remarkably slow to accept a proper share of the cost of mitigating its worst effects.

To argue that modern farming uses excessive inputs to produce unsaleable outputs may be true, but confuses two arguments. There is a strong case for a radical overhaul of the Common Agricultural Policy; but to assume that a 'free market' in agriculture produces a more environmentally sensitive breed of farmer is to fly in the face of North American evidence. Nor, incidentally, does socialist agriculture. As early as 1970, *Pravda* was complaining that the reckless use of chemical pesticides in agriculture was decimating many species of wildlife in the Soviet Union: 'Our woods, gardens and fields are becoming quieter and quieter ...' If we want to preserve tracts of countryside for ecological/aesthetic purposes, let's do so, without confusing that object with agriculture.

That is not to impugn the 'polluter pays' principle. The pollution of lakes and rivers by nitrogeneous run-off and slurries has become a matter of great concern to both fresh- and salt-water biologists. When added to the stress already placed on major water bodies by acid rain and non-agricultural pollution, it can administer the coup-de-grace to an aquatic ecosystem. Steps have been taken in the UK to control slurry effluents, but it is an open question whether they will be enforced vigorously. No such action has been taken on fertiliser run-off, though that is quantitively a far bigger problem. Some polluters pay: far too many do not. Agricultural polluters have a powerful union and well-developed political muscles. It would be a courageous government that made the 'polluter pays' principle stick.

It is time to shift the focus—back to the global. The last two issues I want to raise affect Third World and First World equally. Indeed they are set in areas where the interests of the two collide; and to a degree, it is that collision which endangers the environment of us all.

## TROPICAL MOIST FOREST

Many ecologists regard the tropical moist forests of China, Brazil and Western Central Africa as three of the most important treasure houses of the natural environment. They not only contain an amazing wealth of flora and fauna, they also contribute in three important ways to the survival of the global ecosystem.

They are the lungs of the atmosphere, absorbing carbon dioxide and releasing oxygen. They are the rain-makers of their region and beyond: anyone who has flown over the northern tracts of the Sahara, once a well-watered forest, does not need convincing of the importance of that function. Third, and least well understood, the tropical moist forest is a valuable source of germ plasm. Many biologists now fear that the depletion of the tropical moist forest could seriously affect the security of crop strains throughout the world, as well as rendering more unlikely the discovery of new species of plants with significant economic or medicinal potential.

How and why, then, is the tropical moist forest being depleted? Population pressure plays its part and needs no repetition here. Much more significant are activities such as logging, and the clearing of vast tracts of the forest by international food companies in order to satisfy the market in Europe and, particularly, North America. For example, more than a quarter of Central American forests have been destroyed since 1906 to produce beef. Although some of this was for home consumption, most of it went to the United States—to produce low quality hamburgers and dog food. Official figures attribute 38 per cent of all deforestation of the Brazilian Amazon basin between 1966 and 1975 to cattle ranching. Although no doubt some of the beef was consumed in Brazil, it is not irrelevant that Brazilian beef exports to the United States and the Middle East climbed dramatically in this period.

The position with logging is not greatly different. Some of the timber is used domestically but the valuable hardwoods are exported for use in the furniture, construction and boat building industries in Europe and North America. Logging companies are selective about the trees they take from the forest, and to get the best wood out they have to build roads into the heart of the forest: the road network in a logging concession can cover as much as 20 per cent of the total area. It is thus no surprise to find that in Brazil 27 per cent of deforestation in the Amazon basin is accounted for by highway and logging road construction. It is along these arteries that settlers move in, finishing the clearing that the logging companies have begun, and preventing the roads they have made reverting to forests.

No one knows how fast the tropical moist forest is disappearing. Estimates vary between under 6 and over 20 million hectares per year. The Food and Agricultural Organisation of the UN comes near the lower end of that estimate, reckoning that all tropical forest is disappearing at the rate of 7.3 million hectares per year. As the UN is dependent upon government statistics and governments collude with those who destroy tropical forests, it is probable that the figure is higher, perhaps much higher, than the FAO estimate.

If depletion at this annual rate continues, the mid-term effects—say by the middle of the next century—could be disastrous. For example, the US *Global 2000* report estimates that one million plant and animal species currently found in the tropical forests could be extinct by the end of this century if deforestation continues at the present rate. That would represent a major economic and biological loss which would be irreplaceable and which would leave long-run plant breeding programmes in serious jeopardy.

## PRAYER

Prayer for the natural environment is prayer that humankind may rediscover a wisdom that emphasises the qualities of caretaking rather than exploitation.

To allow the scale of the change that is required to sink in, it would be good to go back to the biblical material and work through it again, reading and praying it against any of the analytical section that came alive for you. There are any number of ways of doing this, but one way is to 'live' in the contrast between the glory that God has created and the desolation that humankind has made it: for example, the contrast between natural forest and trees dying through poisoning; the contrast between running streams filled with an amazing diversity of aquatic life and turgid dead water polluted by agricultural and industrial wastes; the contrast between the natural diversity of plants and the monotony of the corn belt.

As you live in these contrasts, the object is not to be assailed by a paralysing guilt or hopelessness, but by the possibilities of redemption. Go back especially to the passages from Romans and Philippians and ask God to show you through them the possibility of a world transformed.

You may find Paul's image of the whole of creation groaning in labour as it waits to be set free from the consequences of man's selfishness a good starting point for moving on to a deeper, more heart-centred longing for the restoration of covenant and kingdom values in our culture.

That may lead you to look again at the values lived out in your life and the life of your community. Again, ask to be privileged to see what needs to be changed; where, that is, the assumptions, demands and expectations of your community (and define community in any way you like) conflict with the redemption of the natural environment.

As you do that, it is crucial to keep constantly in mind the love God has for your community. It too is waiting for its redemption.

Its solidarity in sin with the rest of us is a fact; but it is not an excuse for drowning in guilt. For Jesus is Lord—and he is setting us free from our guilt to enable us to live in the values of his kingdom.

So where is he calling us? Where, for it is the same question, is he at work in his world to bring about the redemption for which we all long? We are back with the kairos. Where are we being offered moments of decisive opportunity? Through what agencies? You may want to pray for the discernment to see where the Lord of history is taking our history by the scruff of the neck and giving it a good shake.

## ACTION

**1.** Prayer is action; action is prayer. You will want to find a way of incorporating what comes alive for you in the section above in your regular prayer life. But you will want to go on from there. One structured way of doing that would be to make your own list of biblical passages that point to God's creativity in the world, its destruction and its redemption—and then use that material for meditative prayer.

Another approach altogether is to centre your prayer on any of the actions in the following list you decide is right for you. Take that action into the presence of God, in a quiet spirit of offering. Pray particularly for people who oppose or abuse you; for your ability to love them, as well as for their conversion.

**2.** Look again at the liturgy of your church. How does that reflect the work you have been doing in this chapter? Is there room for a more adequate incorporation of the ideas in this chapter in the regular worship, or in an occasional 'special' service?

**3.** What about the teaching ministry of the church? How often are these issues on the agenda? What prevents them being on it more often? Why? Who? What do you and others in your church think about that?

**4.** There are a number of organisations you can join that will keep you in touch with developments. They run from the National Trust to Greenpeace, to Friends of the Earth. Most localities have some kind of local society that covers at least some of the issues. Some are alert and engaged. Others went into a deep sleep long ago and could do with a gentle nudge.

A local solution to the problem of diminishing supplies of firewood. This Indian farmer makes dung cakes to burn as fuel.

**5.** More and more schools and colleges are offering environmentally related courses. Inevitably the quality varies. It could be worth finding out what the policy of your local LEA is and doing anything you can to support teachers and lecturers in these subjects. That support can take a wide variety of forms, from pressure on the LEA for a more adequate level of funding to offers of help with transport for field visits. (Watch the insurance angle; it can be tricky.)

**6.** What about the informal networks in your locality? Chambers of Commerce, Inner Wheel, Rotary...? How open are they to helping their members understand some of the issues—both local and international? How ready are they to play a part in local monitoring (see below)? What do they think about notorious local polluters? (See below again.)

**7.** The local press can often play a major role in changing opinions, especially about local matters. Befriend someone on the local paper and encourage him or her to give proper coverage to environmental issues and to have the guts to raise the real issues.

**8.** Join a local environmental monitoring group if there is one; think about helping to start one if there isn't.

**9.** Protest local polluters and notorious national polluters: for example, the CEGB, NIREX, extractive industries that do not restore the environment when they have finished and do not screen or improve their spoil tips; chemical industries that dump their waste at sea or in rivers; smelters that do not clean their atmospheric emissions.

**10.** Let your local council member know that you are interested in the council's policies and actions on environmental matters: for example, sewage disposal, enforcement of environmental legislation. Ask where he or she stands and encourage public debate about local issues. Local public transport is usually a good opener.

**11.** Use unleaded petrol yourself and try to persuade others to do so. Again, go after the public sector. They ought to be setting an example.

**12.** Are there any environmental improvement schemes in your area, for example, tree planting? Take part if you can. Encourage and congratulate those responsible. Hammer vandals.

**13.** Are there any recycling projects locally? Bottle-banks? Paper collection? What does the council do with its rubbish? Could it not be used more sensibly?

**14.** Let your MP (and any members of the House of Lords, including Anglican bishops) know that there is local interest in these issues. Select one of national (rather than purely local) significance and ask for a statement. Ask to see speeches and questions he or she has made, or ask why they said nothing in debates on relevant issues.

## APPRAISAL

From time to time, it is good to look back at the whole cycle, especially to see how the integration of prayer and action is working out. There is always a danger that we forget that the agenda is God's; that it is his kingdom and his kairos. Very easily the action grips us in its own dynamic, so that we lose any critical distance. Then we get sucked into local or even national power plays. We become objects of history, not the allies of the Lord of history.

In the appraisal, too, it is worth looking at the development of the inner life from the perspective of the growth of the capacity to love. That is not to belittle the role of anger; the careless polluter deserves, perhaps even needs, our anger. But the anger has finally to issue in love, and be undergirded by love. Anger alone will make it more, rather than less, difficult for the person to change.

Appraisal is at least as much a group activity as it is an individual necessity. Let the group—whatever it is, whether church-based or not—talk out how it works as a group. Are the tasks fairly shared? Does everyone feel that their contribution is valued? Do people feel that they matter? Is someone lacking in sensitivity to the shrinking violets? Can they be helped to see that?

These *process* discussions are at least as important as *product* discussions. How are we functioning as a group? Are we making any headway? And if the honest answer to the second question is 'No', a good place to start looking for the reason is in the first question.

That does not imply, of course, that we can expect to be highly effective all the time. Certainly not. In biblical language, we are up against Principalities and Powers, and they are not easily defeated: they have too much to lose. So the appraisal time can be a time for finding and mobilising those resources that the Greeks knew as *hypomone*: grit, stickability, a refusal to let go. Not surprisingly, this was the Christian virtue that St John of Patmos, who knew a lot about struggle and persecution, valued most highly.

# Chapter Three

# COMMUNITY

## REFLECTION ON THE LOVE OF GOD

READ
1 SAMUEL
17:32–52

David said to Saul, 'Let no one lose heart on his account; your servant will go and fight this Philistine'. But Saul answered David, 'You cannot go and fight the Philistine; you are only a boy and he has been a warrior from his youth.'

David said to Saul, 'Your servant used to look after the sheep for his father and whenever a lion or a bear came out and took a sheep from the flock, I used to follow him up and strike him down and rescue it from his mouth; if he turned on me I seized him by the hair at his jaw and struck him down and killed him. Your servant has killed both lion and bear, and this uncircumcised Philistine shall be like one of them, for he has dared to insult the armies of the living God. Yahweh who rescued me from the claws of lion and bear,' David said, 'will rescue me from the power of this Philistine.' Then Saul said to David, 'Go, and Yahweh be with you!'

Saul made David put on his own armour and put a bronze helmet on his head and gave him a breastplate to wear, and over David's armour he buckled his own sword; but not being used to these things David found he could not walk. 'I cannot walk with these,' he said to Saul, 'I am not used to them.' So they took them off again.

He took his staff in his hand, picked five smooth stones from the river bed, put them in his shepherd's bag, in his pouch, and with his sling in his hand he went to meet the Philistine. The Philistine, his shield-bearer in front of him, came nearer and nearer to David; and the Philistine looked at David, and what he saw filled him with scorn, because David was only a youth, a boy of fresh complexion and pleasant bearing. The Philistine said to him, 'Am I a dog for you to come against me with sticks?' And the Philistine cursed David by his gods. The Philistine said to David, 'Come over here and I will give your flesh to the birds of the air and the beasts of the field.' But David answered the Philistine, 'You come against me with sword and spear and javelin, but I come against you in the name of Yahweh Sabaoth, the God of the armies of Israel that you have dared to insult. Today Yahweh will deliver you into my hand and I shall kill you; I will cut off your head, and this very day I will give your dead body and the bodies of the Philistine army to the birds of the air and the wild beasts of the earth, so that all the earth may know that there is a God in Israel, and that all this assembly may know that it is not by sword or by spear that Yahweh gives the victory, for Yahweh is lord of the battle and he will deliver you into our power.'

No sooner had the Philistine started forward to confront David than David left the line of battle and ran to meet the Philistine. Putting his hand in his bag, he took out a stone and slung it and struck the Philistine on the forehead; the stone penetrated his forehead and he fell on his face to the ground. Thus David triumphed over the Philistine with a sling and a stone and struck the Philistine down and killed him. David had no sword in his hand. Then David ran and, standing over the Philistine, seized his sword and drew it from the scabbard, and with this he killed him, cutting off his head.

The Philistines saw that their champion was dead and took to flight.

An important part of one tradition about King David, David the righteous warrior, this story should be read against Colossians 2:14–15. For whatever its original purpose (probably to glorify the king's might in battle), it is still a significant reminder of the religious conviction of Israel that Yahweh the Lord of Hosts protects those who, however inadequately prepared for the task, champion his cause. The central point of the story lies in the contrast between the Philistine who goes to battle fully prepared and equipped but placing his faith in idols—and, we may assume, in his superior strength and technology; and the youthful David whose physical resources are meagre (though perhaps not as wholly inferior as we are invited to infer), but whose faith is in the God of righteousness and justice. Maybe that strikes us as simplistic: even pietistic, for we are conscious of how often the Philistines seem to conquer all

In modern culture, a 'real man' stands out a mile, never eats quiche, and swims through shark-infested waters simply to deliver a box of chocolates to the woman he loves. A Christian understanding of humanity cuts across such popularly-understood standards of power and greatness.

before them in our own world. Yet David's myth played a central role in preparing God's people for David's greatest Son who would allow the contemporary Philistines to do their worst: and still triumph over them.

READ MICAH 3:9–12

Now listen to this, you princes of the House of Jacob,
rulers of the House of Israel,
you who loathe justice
and pervert all that is right,
you who build Zion with blood,
Jerusalem with crime.
Her princes pronounce their verdict for bribes,
her priests take a fee for their rulings,
her prophets make divinations for money.
And yet they rely on Yahweh. They say,
'Is not Yahweh in our midst?
No evil is going to overtake us.'
Because of this, since the fault is yours,
Zion will become ploughland,
Jerusalem a heap of rubble,
and the mountain of the Temple a wooded height.

Typical of many oracles from the eighth century prophets (see, for instance, Jeremiah 22:13–17; Amos 3:9–15), these verses condemn three activities or attitudes which make community impossible and Yahweh a totem. First is straight economic exploitation that finances luxury dwellings for the rich and powerful (vv.9b–10). Second is corruption—of state and Church officials (11a). Third, and to the prophet most scandalous of the three, is the assumption that Yahweh will condone or connive with this kind of behaviour (11b). Since Yahweh is the source of all power and authority, however, he demands that it be used to make possible a quality of relationship that reflects his covenant love for his people. When it is used for personal enrichment and political or ecclesiastical advancement, the judgment is severe. 'The fault is yours' (v.12) and destruction unimaginable to the cocooned rich is declared inevitable.

READ MATTHEW 21:12–17

Jesus then went into the Temple and drove out all those who were selling and buying there; he upset the tables of the money changers and the chairs of those who were selling pigeons. 'According to scripture,' he said, 'my house will be called a house of prayer; but you are turning it into a robbers' den.' There were also blind and lame people who came to him in the Temple, and he cured them. At the sight of the wonderful things he did and of the children shouting, 'Hosanna to the Son of David' in the Temple, the chief priests and the scribes were indignant. 'Do you hear what they are saying?' they said to him. 'Yes,' Jesus answered, 'have you never read this:

*By the mouths of children, babes in arms,*
*you have made sure of praise*?'

With that he left them and went out of the city to Bethany where he spent the night.

It is important not to detach verses 12 and 13 from verses 14–16, for the expulsion of the dealers from the Temple is one of three signs of the imminent in-breaking of the kingdom. The curing of the blind and lame is the second, and the cheers of the children, so shocking to the ecclesiastical authorities, the third. Each is heavy with symbolism.

Many scholars believe that Jesus threw out the dealers less because they were dishonest (he does not charge them with that directly) than because they had encroached into the Temple proper instead of remaining in the outer court. His action thus challenged the authority of the Chief Priest and the Sanhedrin by its implicit accusation of at best irreverence, at worst corruption. On this account Jesus is seeking to restore purity of worship, and with it, respect for just dealing and mutuality.

The blind and the lame are frequent symbols for those who are prevented from 'seeing' the kingdom of God, and those who cannot join in welcoming it. Both infirmities were regarded as punishment for misdeeds, so Jesus' cure is a promise of forgiveness for all who want to be part of the kingdom.

The children repeat the cry of the crowd at the entry into Jerusalem (21:9), thus reinforcing the expectation that 'this prophet, Jesus of Nazareth' is, in some still unclear sense, the one who saves. The kingdom is proclaimed to be imminent, not by those whose function it was to declare God's purposes, but by the children. Like the blind and lame, they are supposedly the least likely to perceive God at work in his world.

READ ACTS 2:42–47

These remained faithful to the teaching of the apostles, to the brotherhood, to the breaking of bread and to the prayers.

The many miracles and signs worked through the apostles made a deep impression on everyone.

The faithful all lived together and owned everything in common; they sold their goods and possessions and shared out the proceeds among themselves according to what each one needed.

They went as a body to the Temple every day but met in their houses for the breaking of bread; they shared their food gladly and generously; they praised God and were looked up to by everyone. Day by day the Lord added to their community those destined to be saved.

While this may be a somewhat idealised account of the life of the early Church, and one moreover written from the contemporary expectation of the imminent return of Christ in glory, it gives us a vivid picture of the ideal of Christian community. Although it is fashionable to fasten on verses 44–45 and extract from them some model of social organisation, it is more pertinent (and less unhistorical) to give prior emphasis to the fourfold description with which St Luke starts this account. The 'teaching' is a persistent theme of the author and refers to Jesus' whole ministry. The apostles taught that Jesus' ministry, death and resurrection proved he was the Son of God whose life on earth had transformed human possibilities. One result of that transformation was the discovery of 'brotherhood' or 'fellowship' among believers—a discovery that made racial, gender, financial or legal divisions between believers no longer pertinent. Sharing bread, goods, worship and care for the poor was now both natural and mandatory. This was symbolised in sharing the common meal of the Lord's Supper and celebrated in common prayers of petition and thanksgiving.

Clearly the early Church lived a new quality of life, one characterised by praise and generosity. No doubt the expectation of the end of all things gave a particular incentive to live out such freedom. As that expectation faded, what happened to the ideal of Christian living?

READ COLOSSIANS 3:9–17

You have stripped off your old behaviour with your old self, and you have put on a new self which will progress towards true knowledge the more it is renewed in the image of its creator; and in that image there is no room for distinction between Greek and Jew, between the circumcised or the uncircumcised, or between barbarian and Scythian, slave and free man. There is only Christ: he is everything and he is in everything.

You are God's chosen race, his saints; he loves you, and you should be clothed in sincere compassion, in kindness and humility, gentleness and patience. Bear with one another; forgive each other as soon as a quarrel begins. The Lord has forgiven you; now you must do the same. Over all these clothes, to keep them together and complete them, put on love. And may the peace of Christ reign in your hearts, because it is for this that you were called together as parts of one body. Always be thankful.

Let the message of Christ, in all its richness, find a home with you. Teach each other, and advise each other, in all wisdom. With gratitude in your hearts sing psalms and hymns and inspired songs to God; and never say or do anything except in the name of the Lord Jesus, giving thanks to God the Father through him.

Another declaration of the shattering effect of the gospel of Jesus Christ, this passage reminds us that belief in Christ and baptism into his body the Church stands many of our prejudices and expectations on their heads. The 'new self' can no longer accept even elementary divisions in the human race: *all* men and women are 'in Christ', but have to discover for themselves the full reality of that astonishing fact. The writer insists, like the fourth Evangelist, that the mark of that reality is love, which he translates (v.12) as compassion, kindness, humility, gentleness, patience and a readiness to forgive. These are, too, the gifts of the Spirit, and will culminate in the peace of Christ.

There is a great danger that we may etherealise this teaching, forcing it into a personalised, internal religiosity. Verse 15 should warn us how distorted a view of Christian life that is. We 'were called together as parts of one body'—a central theme in all of St

Paul's teaching. The characteristics of life together in the Church are to be a foretaste of life together in the redeemed fellowship of the whole created order. No wonder St Paul sees that as a call to thanksgiving (v.15).

READ 1 JOHN 1:5–10

This is what we have heard from him,
and the message that we are
announcing to you:
God is light; there is no darkness in
him at all.
If we say that we are in union with God
while we are living in darkness,
we are lying because we are not living
the truth.
But if we live our lives in the light,
as he is in the light,
we are in union with one another,
and the blood of Jesus, his Son,
purifies us from all sin.

If we say we have no sin in us,
we are deceiving ourselves
and refusing to admit the truth;
but if we acknowledge our sins,
then God who is faithful and just
will forgive our sins and purify us
from everything that is wrong.
To say that we have never sinned
is to call God a liar
and to show that his word is not in us.

This passage points us in the same general direction, but with a special intensity and the characteristic vocabulary of the fourth Gospel. The whole letter is a highly condensed, compact summary of the key ideas of the Gospel and these verses are in many ways a summary of that summary. Light, truth and union with God and each other are the three central ideas. Light is as incompatible with darkness as sin is with the new quality of life Christians are called to live. That quality of life is shown by the truth lived by Jesus—the truth of humble service, of redemptive suffering, of glory, of cross and resurrection. When we allow the love of God to penetrate us as completely as it penetrated Jesus, then we can live at peace with each other, a relationship that frees us to discover in human community the fullness of God's creation.

Here, then, in a very few words packed with meaning and emotional compulsion, is the heart of the Christian gospel. Christ sets us free to become what God created us to be. As we find that to be true, we shall experience it as revolution—as well as revelation.

## ANALYSIS

The Christian vision is one of community. That is to say, we are called to make community in our present environment; and we look for the perfection of community in God's final reign on earth.

Community is, however, a slippery concept. It tends to mean

different things to different people. To some it means holding all things in common. To others it means doing away with hierarchical patterns of decision-making, and to yet others it means sharing respect and affection, as in a close-knit family.

One feature that nearly every concept of community has in common is the valuing of every member of the community. To take an extreme example, L'Arche is a community for mentally handicapped people. They live and work in houses with a roughly equal number of 'assistants', usually younger people who have pledged some years of their lives to L'Arche. It would be easy for the assistants to run the community. They could quickly assess the facts, see what needs doing and make the right decisions. But what would that do to the other members of the community? It would leave them as helpless, disabled onlookers with no voice in the affairs of their own community. To all intents and purposes, they would cease to be effective members of the community at all.

It is for that reason that the founder of L'Arche, Jean Vanier, has insisted from the beginning that the mentally handicapped members of the community be encouraged to take part in all discussions, that their contributions be taken as seriously as anyone else's, and that no decision be taken until all the members of the community feel that they 'own' it. 'And the extraordinary thing is,' says a friend who works in a L'Arche house, 'that it is often the mentally handicapped whose contributions turn out to be the most valuable. Perhaps not the most articulate. Sometimes not even the most logical according to our way of thinking. But the most creative ... It always pays to wait and listen—even to the most unlikely people.'

In this section, I am going to explore four areas of our 'common life' where any notion of community is under threat because we have lost the possibility of listening to all the members of the community. I shall argue that the power to make major and in some cases fundamental decisions lies in the hands of 'the experts' with the result that ordinary people—who together form the great bulk of the community—are left feeling alienated, hopeless and disabled.

That is not how God intended people to be. It is not how he intended human society to operate. But how did he intend it to operate? That is a much debated question. I am not concerned here, however, with exploring particular forms of government to see which is nearest to the Christian ideal: that is too ambitious an undertaking. Rather, I see a sign of the times in the rising sense of powerlessness, helplessness, despair and ultimately cynicism of people whose value as members of the community is denied by

Big business buildings, New York. Decisions made here have a direct impact on countries and populations across the world.

their exclusion from processes of decision-making in areas that directly affect their lives.

And I want to suggest that this issue has a kairos quality about it because of what the denial of value is doing to people. I refer not only to all the evils of our culture associated with this sense of alienation—from drugs, to promiscuity, to vandalism, to a deep seated cynicism that meets denial of value with denial of value. At a deeper level, the concentration of influence and power in fewer and fewer hands deprives the majority of men and women of the possibility of exercising responsibility for the world in which they live.

They are thus denied the opportunity of fulfilling their vocation to be co-creators with God. For that vocation is universal. It is not confined to statesmen or industrialists or research scientists. It is part of what it means to be human. It is a privilege of the human condition. To fashion a society which is increasingly split between the decision-makers and the decision-takers is thus to fashion a society that is divided between the human and the sub-human. That is a blasphemy because it denies the glory of God's creativity in each member of the human race.

It is also inefficient and impoverishing. For the experts cannot know everything there is to be known. They are the captives of their own ways of thinking, their own disciplines and ideologies. It was that realisation that led Mao-Zedong to insist that his cadres be taught to 'learn from the People'. And from the other end of the political spectrum, the World Bank has begun to learn the practical value of encouraging the participation of ordinary people in the planning of projects—even large, complex projects which will affect their lives. 'If we'd had the sense to do this twenty years ago,' one Senior Vice President said, 'we could have saved a lot of money and a lot of embarrassment.'

Most of us are neither Chinese cadres nor officials of the World Bank. Nor are we those whom they seek to serve. We find ourselves caught in the web of an increasingly complex and fascinating world, but one in which decisions which closely affect us may be taken at the furthest end of the web and be communicated to us through a long chain of threads and nodes. When those decisions reach us—and we see their ramifications—we can do nothing. We have become victims. Objects. Human chess pieces to be moved for the sake of some grand strategy we neither comprehend nor influence. We shrug our shoulders and say: 'Well, that's life. Can't be helped. Someone has to decide. Expect they have their reasons ...' The web has caught us inextricably.

If that seems far-fetched or over-blown, consider the case of Jim Chapman. Jim worked in a factory near London making hydraulic pumps. He had worked in that factory for thirty-two years, all his working life. He had become line supervisor, and what Jim didn't know about making hydraulic pumps wasn't worth knowing. He ran a tight ship, friendly but firm, and was respected by both management and workers on the line. 'You always know where you are with Jim,' they said.

Jim's firm was taken over by an international business based in Newark, New Jersey. Like other employees he was assured it would make no difference. For a time it didn't. Then North Sea oil began to flow—and the price of oil was raised by OPEC. Sterling became a strong currency. Its value rose—and rose.

So Jim's pumps became more and more expensive in the United States. 'No alternative,' they said when they told Jim they were shutting the factory. Certainly there was no alternative for him. He's still unemployed ... The web had caught him.

Jim's story raises the first theme of this chapter: the concentration of economic power. I start with that because it is the aspect of the subject with which most of us come into contact most frequently. In some ways it is the most overt form of powerlessness we, like Jim, experience. That will, however, lead us on to three other areas: powerlessness in politics; powerlessness in information; and powerlessness with respect to the executive branch (i.e. in the Civil Service and other forms of executive authority). In each section we will explore why power has become concentrated, in whose hands it is concentrated and what that concentration does to 'ordinary' men and women.

## CONCENTRATION OF ECONOMIC POWER

> When Adam delved and Eve span
> Who was then the gentleman?

The old revolutionary doggerel has its point. It is romantic to look back to a golden age when economic and financial power were shared equally enough to make talk of community possible, but changes in technology and methods of economic organisation have only accelerated a process that was already well advanced in the days of Benjamin Franklin and Adam Smith. Those changes work in three dimensions.

The first is size. Franklin and Smith were familiar with a scale of production little above that of a workshop. In general, farms tended to employ more people than industrial firms. Not only did the new technologies in textiles, metal production and then engineering change that in the nineteenth century but the development of the assembly line in the early twentieth century changed it more radically still. For the nature of the technology and the way it came to be exploited meant that bigger implied cheaper. The age of economies of scale had dawned.

Now that has an immediate consequence. If bigger means cheaper, it also means fewer. There is only room for a few motor manufacturers or ship builders or iron works.

By the end of World War I, the logic of that was well on the way to working itself out at the national level. By the end of World War II, the time had come to allow it to work itself out at the international level. The slow and painful approach to freer world trade *was* slow and painful precisely because free trade means fewer, larger plants. So the British motorcycle industry disappeared. So did a host of assembly industries, exactly those in which economies of scale are largest—from radios to refrigerators; from pocket calculators to aircraft.

Initially countries like the United States and the original six-member EEC, who have huge internal markets, could benefit from this, using their home markets as a base from which to extract the economies of scale necessary to undercut countries with smaller markets. The US aircraft industry is a classic case; the Italian domination of the white goods market is another.

But the 1960s saw new players enter the game—Japan, then South Korea, Taiwan, Brazil, the so-called NICs (Newly Industrialised Countries). They built bigger plants for world markets—

from scratch. The number of producers of mass consumption assembly goods contracted again—not least because American and European producers realised that the only way they would survive in the world market place was by getting together. Again, the motor industry illustrates the point.

It leads us, too, to the second dimension. A defensive strategy, again well illustrated in the motor industry though by no means confined to it, was what came to be known as the globalisation of production. Huge producers like Ford or General Motors could improve their capacity to compete with Toyota and Nissan of Japan or, emerging in the 1980s, Hyundai of South Korea, if they could have great flexibility to switch production from one country to another to take advantage of tax rates, tariffs, labour and material costs.

Along with the concentration of production, there thus went the separation of central decision making (the HQ) from production (the works). Almost by definition, in the case of globalised production, the two functions would be on two continents, separated not only by distance but by culture, ethos, language, style and work practices. Perhaps inevitably those in 'the works' saw those at HQ as 'them'—faceless, unfeeling manipulators concerned only with the bottom line. On the other side, under the competitive pressures of the last twenty years a small executive committee of senior managers in Newark, NJ or Dusseldorf or Leeds had neither the capacity nor the incentive to know and care about the details of each of several dozen plants, much less of each of several tens of thousands of employers. Pressure had brought alienation.

There is however a further—and more profound—sense in which that was true. And that takes us to the third dimension.

The emergence of the joint stock company during the latter years of the industrial revolution in Britain was the most important and least recognised technical advance of the whole period. It allowed individuals to subscribe capital to industrial companies but limited their liability to the amounts subscribed if the company subsequently failed.

As a way of raising large sums of money quickly it has been outstandingly successful. But at the heart of the notion of the joint stock company lies the crucial separation of control and ownership. For the subscriber of capital yielded his control to the directors who in turn passed day to day management to managers.

As industrial enterprises have become larger, more international, and more complex, so the gaps between shareholder, director and manager have become ever greater. Nor has that been reversed by the fact that the number of shareholders (in relation, for example, to turnover) has tended to decrease as larger and larger portions of the capital of the companies concerned are owned by institutions rather than by individuals.

Typically today a large trans-national corporation will have as much as 80 per cent of its shareholding owned by a modest number of institutions such as insurance companies, pension funds and investment trusts. It will have a very small number of directors in relation to the scale and complexity of its operations—probably no more than twenty. And it will have a huge sub-structure of managers spread throughout the world.

The directors cannot possibly be in touch with every aspect of every subsidiary throughout the world. They are dependent for the flow of information that reaches them on the managers they are supposed to control. They fall back on specific numerical indicators of performance, for example, turnover per employee; profit as a percentage of capital employed; profit as a percentage of sales. Statistics become the essence of management. And the key statistic is inevitably—since that is the duty of the director to the shareholder—profit per unit of capital employed. It is that figure which every director watches like a hawk.

But who elects the directors? In theory, the shareholders. But the shareholders are predominantly large institutions, investing money on behalf of a large number of clients—savers, pensioners, annuitants. Such institutions compete amongst themselves. He gets the business who shows the best return. In choosing directors of the companies in which they invest, hungry hawks are preferred to reflective doves.

Most institutions, however, prefer not to 'interfere' with the companies in which they invest. It can, however, happen that the relevant investment managers from only three or four institutions can bring informal pressure on the directors—sometimes only a small minority of the directors—in order to bring about a change in company policy. Other shareholders will not even be informed of the approaches that have been made. Neither the individual shareholder of the company concerned, nor the client of the institution, will have been consulted over the affairs of the company.

If the power of individual shareholders to control the company is deficient, where does final authority lie? It does not lie with employees. Spread through many countries with very different legal frameworks, cultural backgrounds and patterns of aspiration, it is exceedingly difficult for them to influence a multinational company: they may indeed find it difficult to influence the manager of their local subsidiary. Why don't they get together? Because traditionally labour has been organised either by craft or, in Japan, by plant. The international organisation of labour according to employer has not yet emerged. There have been some signs that it may do so, but in their ability to switch operations from one country to another, to invest here and disinvest there, the large multinational corporations hold a lot of the cards in their hands.

If neither shareholders nor employees nor organised labour can exercise power over these giant companies, we are back with the original question. Where does control lie? Who can take final responsibility for one of the most fundamental forces in our community?

Clearly not, in any sense, the whole community. Even governments are largely powerless on key issues like investment, employment and choice of technology. Nor, despite the rhetoric that 'the consumer is king', can consumers usually affect company policy in those critical areas. (Which is not to deny the influence consumers can bring on very specific, easily defined and marginal-to-the-main-business issues, like trading with South Africa.) No, the truth is that this huge productive machine on which as employees, investors and consumers we all rely is in fact controlled by a smaller and smaller number of people accountable—in fact, rather than in theory—to a smaller and smaller number of institutional investment managers—unelected, unrepresentative, unaccountable, invisible, sometimes even untraceable.

If we put those three dimensions together—scale, globalisation, and non-accountability—we may have even more sympathy with Jim Chapman who led us off on this enquiry. For to return to him for a moment, to whom can Jim look for redress—less in a financial and/or legal sense than in a moral sense? If he were able to trace and tackle the chairman of the American parent company, what would the chairman say? 'I'm under pressure to perform. I had some institutional managers and their brokers round last week and they said they would dump our stock if things don't look up. Or dump me. So I've got to cut costs ...' And the brokers would say: 'Sure we told him to get off his butt. Our clients will soon go elsewhere if he can't deliver ...' And the clients would say: 'It's nothing to do with me. I didn't know anything about your company ... but I do need a decent pension.'

Poor Jim. No wonder he spits if you mention the word community.

In the last section we did not mention one avenue Jim might have tried. He might have gone to his local (or possibly even a national) newspaper. Supposing they had run an exposé on an American multinational bullying a small British firm? Suppose they had urged their readers to boycott all the multinational's products? Suppose they had kept the pressure up with a series of tear-jerking articles on Jim's unemployed colleagues? It probably would not have persuaded the US parent to change its mind: but it would certainly have ensured that next time a similar decision confronted senior management, the chairman would have urged extreme caution—whatever the pressures from the institutional managers and their brokers.

The power of the media is not only great: it is much more subterranean and insidious than the crude 'campaign' type journalism on which we have just been fantasising. As we will see in the chapter on militarism, not only our 'news' but our ways of thinking, our vocabulary, our interpretative framework, are all deeply affected, and in some cases wholly determined, by our exposure to the media. Nor are even the most sophisticated of us proof against this. We may imagine that we can discount 'what you read in the papers'. In fact the papers, the radio, the television, the magazines play such a central role in the creation of our culture that, first, they have a direct if unconscious effect on each of us; and second, they heavily influence the intellectual environment in which we all form our opinions, test our prejudices and modify our assumptions. It is as vain for someone to imagine he is unaffected by the media as it is for a fish to think it is unaffected by water.

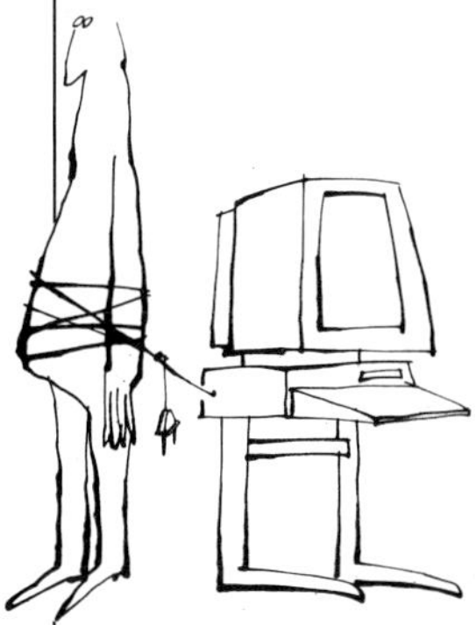

Which makes questions about control of the media as important as they are uncomfortable. By control I mean something wider than ownership, central though that may be. I include editorial control, influence from advertisers, from non-elected watchdogs, from pressure groups: all that subtle, shifting interplay of interests that together determines what I read in my newspaper or watch on television.

If we go back to our original discussion of community, the big question is this: how is the consensus determined within which the media operate (about, for instance, what is 'news' or how a particular news item is interpreted)? Is it responsive to the community, or is it imposed by particular interests for their own ends?

This is a large and widely fought question. I want to make only four points.

**1.** The more widely ownership and editorial control are spread, the less likely is it that one particular interest will come to dominate the culture of the media. In that respect, current trends are conflicting. Critics from the left point to the ambitions of latter day press barons like Maxwell, Murdoch and Packer, who are building up multi-media international networks and are thereby acquiring great power to determine output. In Australia and the United Kingdom, you can read a newspaper, browse through a magazine, watch television and listen to a radio programme without being aware that the same one man could, if he so desired, ensure that you received the same message. More insidiously, the same individual could ensure that you did *not* receive a message he was anxious to suppress. In the United States, there are laws that prevent *local* monopolies of the media (so that the same owner cannot control press and TV) but it is a moot point whether such legislation achieves its real objective.

The same critics point to the close links between these press magnates and the international business community—themselves, as we have already seen, beneficiaries of the concentration of economic power. Sometimes those links are so close they are embodied in one man. 'Tiny' Rowland owns the UK's most prestigious Sunday newspaper, as well as a daily and a London evening paper. He controls, through Lonrho PLC, a vast international commercial empire from diamonds to cattle, from sugar to motorcar trading. Despite constitutional safeguards to prevent it, he plays a key role in shaping his newspapers' editorial policy, not least on events in Africa, the home of most of his assets.

The Left thus has a serious point which no one who thinks community is important can afford to ignore. But it needs to be put in a wider context. The 'information revolution' is about choice. Some of the wealthier parts of the US are already saturated with choice of radio and television, the media which give the majority of Americans the biggest part of their knowledge of current affairs. Direct satellite broadcasting systems will soon ensure that that is true throughout the rich world. Although no doubt in many countries—though some will legislate to prevent it—some of the channels available through satellite relay will be owned/controlled/heavily influenced by newspaper or news service owners, it is unlikely that any will achieve sufficiently broad a grip to stifle alternative views.

The Left has an answer to this point. The question, they say, is not one of direct control: it is rather the creation of a culture, a set of norms, of expectations, of career patterns. Only the committed or the foolhardy can afford to break free of these norms. The 'community' values of the media will continue to be the values of the business 'community'.

We cannot pursue this debate further. We have taken it far enough to see that we are a long, long way from the ideals of L'Arche. The underprivileged, disadvantaged, ill-equipped of our society are seldom heard. Nor are the 'ordinary', the average, the commonplace and the unimportant. Their views, their fears, their priorities are neither news nor features. They are, or are assumed to be, the sand in which more significant fingers can write.

**2.** Because information is, and is increasingly seen to be, an access route to power, those in our societies who are already at a disadvantage are likely to find themselves squeezed even further from this route. The poor do not have and are unlikely to acquire access to information that allows them to challenge the privileges of those who have already acquired it. We can see that when we look at those who have access to electronically stored data. The poor do not in general have services such as Ceefax and Prestel, that is, information services stored in central computers but accessed through domestic television. Likewise, the poor cannot use home banking systems, home shopping systems, and although they have in theory rights to information about them stored on personal and private data banks, very few of those who are computer illiterate have the confidence or means to exercise that right. It now costs £15—nearly half the weekly dole—to see one's computerised medical file.

Furthermore, many commentators expect that as more and more information is made available mainly through computers or computer-related telecommunications, so the bias against the poor and the computer illiterate will intensify. For the technology changes so fast that to keep up with it—that is, to be able to use it effectively—two things are required: sufficient money to buy the necessary hardware and sufficient time and skill to learn how to use it.

In this sense, then, the electronic information revolution is anti-community. It squeezes out those who cannot master the technology on which it depends. At the moment, it may seem of no great significance that half our national community is deprived of home banking and home shopping. True. But as information services become more interactive, as they already are doing in some specialised fields, so those who cannot interact are robbed of voice. And as interactive systems are applied increasingly to serious issues (and not only to quiz shows or light entertainment) that deprivation takes on an increasingly insidious, even sinister, character. In San Francisco in 1986 an interactive AIDS advisory service was declared a huge success, until it was realised that some of the most at-risk groups—for example, drug dependent prostitutes—could not afford the technology. A major 'community medicine' initiative had missed one of the most vulnerable groups in the community.

**3.** When we turn the focus from the domestic poor to the international poor, the contrast and its implications become even more striking. Ten nations own 80 per cent of the world's telecommunications media. The whole of the developing world accounts for less than 8 per cent. To put it crudely, the developing world is in danger of missing out on a technical, social and industrial revolution that is at least equivalent to the Industrial Revolution in the eighteenth century. Here are three very different implications:

> **1.** Because they do not have the information technology, developing countries find themselves hampered in their economic and financial dealings with those who have it. When they are trying to sell their primary commodities on open international markets, when they are trying to protect themselves against variations in exchange rates, they find they are in a position equivalent to fighting a modern war with pikes and cutlasses.
>
> **2.** Their own broadcasting authorities are outgunned, even within their own national borders, by satellite relayed material from the superpowers. In some particularly repressive countries, that might be considered a benefit. In the general case, however, it cannot be desirable that those who have an interest in destabilising or undermining a regime should have unlimited access to the population of that regime on an entirely non-reciprocal basis. Ask Nicaraguans what they think of *Voice of America*.
>
> **3.** In so far as the new information technology represents the starting point for a new production technology—through computerised design and manufacture, for example—the lack of capacity in the developing world to manage its own information technology represents an exclusion from that productive technology. Half of 1 per cent of the research and development expenditure of transnational corporations is carried on in developing countries. In other words, the new productive technology which presents great potential for increasing human productivity will be in the ownership and control of the already rich. Access to that technology will not be given to developing countries: they will have to buy it. Or go without it. For the poorest countries the latter will be the only option. Their relative poverty can only increase.

As the information revolution grows and becomes a part of normal life for some, it squeezes out those who cannot use the new technologies. The poor, shut out of the electronic world, become more disadvantaged.

If we take these three implications together, we see that the power that comes from information is as unequally distributed internationally as it is nationally. For Christians the whole world is called to discover community. As long as two-thirds of the world's population is excluded from information technology and the power it bestows, global community will remain a romantic parrot-cry. The L'Arche analogy looks like the reverse of reality.

## THE CONCENTRATION OF POLITICAL POWER

Sir Winston Churchill had this to say during a speech in the House of Commons: 'Everybody here has private interests. Some are directors of companies. Some own property which may be affected by legislation which is passing ... and there are those people who come to represent public bodies, particular groups of a non-political nature in the general sense ... We are not supposed to be an assembly of gentlemen who have no interests of any kind and no association of any kind ...' Precisely so. The question that has come to dominate discussions of distribution of political power, however, is whether the 'interests' and 'associations' with which politicians are linked acquire an undue leverage in the legislative process.

For it is a clear trend on both sides of the Atlantic that pressure groups have become increasingly influential. The reasons for that, however, are very different in the United Kingdom than the United States. In the UK two features of the British political process seem to have played a key role. First is the very fact that, whatever Sir Winston Churchill may have said, the British House of Commons is indeed 'an assembly of gentlemen'. That is to say, the amateur quality of British politics remains one of its most cherished traditions. The House sits after lunch, so that Members may follow their 'real' professions during the morning. Members have no professional research staff. Until very recently, many did not even have full-time secretaries. Only the most senior have proper office accommodation.

The need for members of Parliament to have access to well-researched information with a minimum of expenditure of time and effort on their behalf has opened the way to pressure groups. That way has been made smoother by the development of Select Committees (an idea borrowed from Congress) which gives pressure groups an ideal platform from which to launch their particular point of view. Coincidentally, the development of Select Committees in the 1970s gave those MPs who sit on them an incentive to acquire the kind of information that pressure groups and lobbies put into their hands—so that they could cross-question opposing

Anyone can buy shares—if they have the money. But who controls the companies in which they are investing?

A crowd is not a community, but it can become one. A major challenge to modern Christianity is to break down the walls that divide individuals and groups in society, and to create true community.

pressure groups the more effectively.

In the United States, the growth of lobbies has a longer tradition. One reason is that the remoteness of legislators in Washington from much of the rest of the country meant that people who had a particular axe to grind had to have someone resident in Washington to grind it for them. It was perhaps the reforming zeal of President John Kennedy, elected in 1960, which gave the greatest boost to pressure groups in the United States. For now liberal pressure groups on such issues as the environment, women's rights and, above all, civil rights for blacks had the chance to be heard.

Equally, however, the alleged assault by John Kennedy on the steel industry had the immediate effect of galvanising the business community into organising themselves to resist such attacks. In 1963, for example, President Eisenhower emerged from retirement to rally businessmen behind the Republican party:

> Businessmen now have to do a little waking up. Businessmen can no longer be sure that there are well-designed and well-observed limits beyond which the government will not go.

A year later the Business and Industry Political Action Committee was formed with the precise intention of ensuring that conservative politicians were sponsored to stand for elected office. Although the constitution forbade the practice of companies making contributions to campaigns of politicians, the prohibition was totally ignored—as the Select Committee on the Presidential Campaign Activities discovered when it investigated the Watergate scandal.

Accordingly, after Watergate the activities of the pressure groups—especially those associated with business and industrial interests—were put on a more regular, that is to say, legal, footing. Pressure groups of all sorts, of Left and Right, had to find out how to play pluralist politics: that is, to accept the outcome of an election and then work hard to get the message across to the powers that be. The number of corporation lobbyists working in Washington doubled between 1975 and 1980. In their work, it is money, contracts, access to the media, information, that are the stuff of success. Business and industrial interests have these assets on a scale that leaves 'alternative' groups far behind. The sad story of the Environmental Protection Act is typical of the result. Weakened in Congress, it was subsequently emasculated by the member of the Administration, James Watt, who was supposed to implement it.

The power of the lobby, then, has increased. And the power of the business lobby has increased most. But what of the lobbies that work for peace and justice: from Shelter and the Child Poverty Action Group in the UK to Bread for the World and Greenpeace in the US? Doesn't their increased activity, access to legislators, and leverage bring great gains to the uninfluential, voiceless and disempowered?

Certainly the number and possibly the effectiveness of such lobbies has increased markedly on both sides of the Atlantic. We need, however, to approach an assessment of their effectiveness in giving voice to the marginalised, those on the fringes of community, with great care. For, as we have already seen, lobbies need resources, not only financial resources, but resources of influence and access. In general, then, those segments of society already *relatively* well-endowed with such resources are able to establish and maintain more effective lobbies than those without them. The contrast between the women's and homeless lobbies in the UK make this point.

Finally, what of the Church as lobby? In the UK it might be assumed that the Church (especially the Anglican Church) is well placed to bring legitimate pressure to bear on behalf of those who are otherwise squeezed out of the legislative process. There is a semi-formal group of Christian MPs in the House of Commons which meets regularly with Church leaders. And there are twenty-six senior Anglican bishops in the House of Lords. Constitutionally, then, the Church (again, particularly the Anglican Church, the established Church of the land) is, by comparison with any other country in the world not excluding Italy, in a remarkably privileged position. What is the record?

One can certainly find individual bishops, occasionally even Archbishops, who have made courageous, sometimes prophetic, speeches in the House of Lords: Durham on the crisis in the North East; Birmingham on abortion; Oxford on homelessness; London on education; Canterbury on inequality. That is worth doing and is, on occasion, done with a high degree of professional skill. Likewise in the Commons, Christian MPs have sometimes worked hard to see that a Bill is put through the House. The best recent example was a Church Measure enabling women to be ordained as Deacons. Much background lobbying, careful preparation and two excellent speeches from the floor of the House ensured a massive majority on an issue that many saw as one of justice—and therefore of community.

Praise where praise is due. But in general one will look in vain to see the Church using its great political leverage on behalf of those on the edges of our community. It is deeply shaming that the best orchestrated, most professionally competent and most energetic campaign that the British churches, led by the British Council of Churches, have mounted in two decades was on Sunday trading—and this at a time when more people have become homeless; more people have become permanently unemployed; more people the victims of racial attacks than at any time since 1945. It is no less shaming to discover that the second most effective Church lobby was on the issue of the taxation of Church assets.

On both sides of the Atlantic, special interest groups may be led by Church dignitaries and even have semi-official or even total backing from a particular denomination. The 'Right to Life' campaign with its support from the Roman Catholic Church hierarchy is one example that is, in essence, common to both the US and UK. In many of these cases, however, (and the 'Right to Life' is a fair example) the opposing lobby can also claim some Church support.

And that is the nub of the issue. For reasons that need no rehearsal here, Christians can usually be found on both sides of a political argument. Even on issues of domestic and global poverty or on first strike nuclear capability, there is no one 'Church view'. Except, therefore, on very limited and institutionally-selfish issues, the Church is not and is unlikely to become an effective advocate.

If community is to be enhanced and protected in the name of Christ, it will be by groups of Christians making common cause with others who may have no overtly Christian motivation. And that very alliance can already be a first fruit of the community we seek and hope for.

## INSTITUTIONAL POWER

Recall for a moment Jim Chapman. Faced with a crisis in his life—redundancy with little chance of new employment—to whom could he turn? Those who made a decision that was for him disastrous were physically, emotionally and functionally far away.

It was that chasm that Jim found hardest to deal with. 'I feel like a pawn in someone else's chess game,' was how he put it.

The result of the concentration of economic, political and informational power, and of the increasing complexity of social life, has been that more of us find ourselves in Jim's position on more issues more frequently. Over a wider set of encounters we find ourselves dealing with an administrative system which is not only impersonal, but opaque, distant, confusing and highly complex. In medicine, education, law, employment, planning, pensions, even something as 'normal' as registering a life or a death, we come up against the power of institutions and administrative systems that we find hard or impossible to manage.

The result is paradoxical. What is designed to be a demonstration of the community's care for all its members—unemployment benefit, for example—becomes a procedure by which the beneficiaries' exclusion from the community is emphasised.

Consider the average applicant for state assistance, whether in the US or the UK. He comes to the point of access to the welfare system with only a hazy idea of his entitlement and the procedures through which he has to pass in order to secure his entitlement in full. On the other side of the window, he is faced with a clerk who, whether literally or metaphorically, has at his fingertips a computer-based information system that will give him in great detail, information about the claimant, the system of benefits and the hoops through which the claimant must pass in the process of making his claim, Quite apart from the differences, in terms of present security and self image between the two actors involved, there is a structural gap that reinforces the claimant's sense of inferiority and powerlessness—of being a pawn in someone else's game.

That is the most obvious example of the way in which institutional power conflicts with Christian notions of community. More insidious and much more widespread is the impact of administrative law on each of us. Administrative law is that body of rules and regulations made by non-elected (and therefore non-accountable) bodies as they carry out the functions delegated to them by the legislature. The scope of administrative law is vast: from driving regulations to water supply; from the ways schools work to the way courts work. The case of Joan Hardy will illustrate what it means to the individual.

Joan was found guilty of embezzlement in 1980 and was sentenced to seven years imprisonment, a sentence that even a hostile press considered harsh. After she had served two and a half years of her sentence, she was eligible for parole, and was accordingly eventually brought before a local Review Committee. As an intelligent woman, she expected that she would be given access to the papers which the (lay) members of the Review Committee had before them. She was not. After some introductory pleasantries, she was asked whether she thought she was ready for parole and what she would do if she were granted it. From the line of subsequent questioning, it became apparent that the members of the Committee had received highly negative reports on her conduct in prison, which Joan put down to the fact that she had reported a senior warder for victimising a fellow prisoner. Her application for parole was refused and Joan was powerless to appeal, to know the reasons why, or to challenge the 'evidence' which led to this decision.

As a leading critic of the system has put it, '... all depends upon what is on the files. Now in a world like that of the prison, which is dominated not merely by security but by the overwhelming atmosphere of *secrecy* that can often govern the most trivial bureaucratic operations, what gets on to the files will seldom, if ever, be scrutinised in the light of common day.' Professor Morris goes on to quote the words of a former Chairman of the Parole Board: 'In these reports, the comments and advice of the Prison Service loom large ... All levels of prison staff contribute to these assessments ... But the Parole Board attach particular significance to those who have close and continuing contact with prisoners—namely, the landing and wing officers and the training staff.'

It is easy to see why Joan's application was refused. It is also easy to see why many prisoners (around 10 per cent of those eligible) have so lost confidence in the system that they refuse even to apply. Better to serve a full sentence, they imply, than be re-sentenced by so arbitrary and unjust a procedure.

Of course the workings of the parole system in the UK is only one—and a rather specialist—example of administrative law at

The average British DHSS office symbolises the way the powerless in society are treated by institutional authority. Filling out impersonal forms, being interviewed through a thick Perspex screen, waiting hours for your turn in depressing surroundings—all emphasise the claimant's lack of importance in the eyes of the system.

work. But it highlights the nature of that law: heavily loaded against the applicant; more responsive to paper than to persons; rigidly bureaucratic; neglectful of the elementary rules of evidence; denying appeal and the right of advocacy.

It is, in short, a system that is hard to square with any biblical concept of community, justice, righteousness or love.

## CONCLUSION

I have argued in this section that one of the leading features of our society is that power is becoming increasingly concentrated in the hands of a few—a few who are neither elected by nor accountable to the community at large. I have suggested that this process leaves most people in our society feeling excluded, alienated and unable to exercise their proper responsibilities for the wellbeing of the community of which they are a part.

I have also suggested that there are deep-seated reasons why this process of concentration is likely to continue. The nature of productive technology; the nature of our economic organisation; the electronic information revolution; and the established interests of those who control 'the system' all point in that direction.

It is the effect of this process on those who pay its highest cost which constitutes the kairos. Most obviously the victims are those who find their lives ruined through no fault of their own, without even the possibility of protest to those who have made the key decisions. The Jims. The Joans. And the millions of people for whom they stand proxy.

There are, however, two other groups who have half-emerged in the course of this chapter and who must now be highlighted. The first comprises those who acquire power and influence from the rest of us. They are the minor victims. Like the rich and the law-keepers in the Gospels, they are the unwitting slaves of values and spiritual perspectives that make it hard for them to enter or recognise the kingdom of God. We identify the concentration of power as a sign to be taken prophetically not only because of what it does to Jim and Joan, but because of what it does to those who victimise them.

Second, between victim and victimiser lie the great majority of the rest of us. We are neither chairmen of international banks nor prisoners denied parole. We are ordinary people, leading an ordinary life doing ordinary things. But we are called into an extraordinary faith.

The British welfare state was established to care for the individual...

And that faith is that Christ died to save the whole world from its greed, its power-lust, its self-service, its wilful blindness to the

PUSH

splendour of the kingdom he seeks to establish. In so far as we allow ourselves to become pawns in someone else's game we refuse to give an adequate response to his death. For the only game we can legitimately play is Christ's. If we perceive that fundamental social processes are standing in the way of Christ's reign on earth, we have no alternative but to protest; to sound warnings; to construct alternatives; to do all in our power to distance ourselves from those processes and their agents. There can be no compromise: no trade-off.

That is why the 'new' community movement is so significant. In all its complexities and many-sidedness, it is a sign of rebellion. It looks for new ways of making decisions; new ways of producing a livelihood; new ways of including the excluded.

## PRAYER

Prayer for this area is that we may rediscover what it means to live responsibly in a quality of relationship with each other that reflects the love of God for his people. As the concentration of power and influence marginalises more and more people domestically and internationally—so that they often react negatively and destructively to what they experience as their own dehumanisation—we look for a vision of a society that can value and incorporate all its members.

Without triggering a disabling guilt, it might be well to start by looking at the way in which we encourage or disable the less articulate and more introvert to take part in the communities of which we are members—family, office, school, factory, church, locality, club, pub. As we operate in those communities, do we enable others to make their contribution, to feel that they have something to offer, to become integrated members of the group—or are we more interested in protecting our own position, using our influence and authority to impose our will, ensuring that we reach the 'right' decision irrespective of the process by which we get there?

Those may be hard, even painful questions. But it is only when we face those inner drives in each of us which make true community impossible that we shall begin to understand the spiritual forces behind the social processes that we have been examining in this chapter. For the point is not that bankers, corporation bosses, media people, newspaper owners and all those who apply administrative law are wicked, craven or evil; it is rather that they find themselves in positions (all right: perhaps force themselves into positions) where the unredeemed part of themselves—that they share with us—has such scope for damaging true community. If we were in their boots, are we sure that things would be discernibly different?

And that should put us in touch with the spiritual forces—what St Paul calls the Powers and Principalities—that constantly seek to atomise humanity, to smash it into bite-size pieces the more readily to engorge it. Most of those spiritual forces will, I suspect, already be familiar to us under different hats: greed, fear, pride, self-centredness, the lust to dominate.

Prayer then becomes pitting our puny spiritual energies against these immensely strong and destructive forces. We do that fearfully—until we remember that we can call in aid the strength of the love of the risen Christ. However alone we may feel and however inadequate to the task, we can cheerfully 'take on' those dangerous dragons, because we know of a superior strength that will defeat them.

It is for that reason that the 'Christus Victor'—the triumphant Christ—is so essential a theme in prayer, even though it is now temporarily out of fashion. If we see through the veil of current events and trends to the centre of the kairos, well may we quail. For at the centre there is a mighty battle being fought out, a battle that St Paul and St John the Divine were familiar with. It is the same battle today: the battle that is between the liberating love of God and the enslaving dominance of the ego. If all we see is the battle, the endless bloody struggle that constantly dehumanises men and women and makes it impossible for them to enjoy the quality of life that God longs to give them ... well, we shall be tempted to give up. We therefore need constantly to remind ourselves and each other that Christ has won, is winning, and will go on winning. In the end, nothing, nothing can separate us from the love of God.

But earth it. Flights of mystical vision are right for those who have the inner discipline and experience to return to earth and plant their feet firmly on the ground. So try to put the cosmic struggle and the final victory of Christ in the context of what you see going on around you. Where is community being curtailed or destroyed? By what processes? Who is being marginalised, squeezed out of full participation in the moulding of their own environment? Try to enter those situations as you pray for the transformation of our individualised lives into true community.

## ACTION

**1.** An obvious place to start is in the church and the community it is supposed to be. Perhaps no more central—and energy-demanding—an activity will ever present itself than making your local worshipping group a community in the fullest sense of that word. Clearly it is a task that can claim a logical priority. What right have any of us Christians to demand of other social formations that they reach a quality of relationship that we discover to be beyond us?

How to do it? There are no easy answers. Four areas are worth looking at as starting points: the use of authority; the style of decision-making and communication; opportunities for interaction, especially amongst those who might be expected to find interaction difficult (for example, across the generations, or ethnic origins or class backgrounds); the sharing of what is genuinely common in the community and the gradual enlargement of what is so perceived.

These, to repeat, are no more than starting points. They will require a lot of work and perhaps some painful conversations before they can be formed into action plans ... but we always need to remember that *we* cannot force community on to other people. That is one mark of its perplexing nature. All we can do is to offer, to share a vision, to give opportunity—and to pray. Maybe that is where we need to start. My own experience, limited as it is, is that when a congregation takes its own community life seriously enough to pray about it regularly and in a disciplined way, things begin to happen.

**2.** Apart from trying to create community in the worshipping congregation, we can try to create community in the neighbourhood, or at least encourage the existing community-makers, from the caring publican to the secretary of the Cricket Club or the youth group. To let them know that they are valued, to help them see what they are doing in a wider perspective than they might have appreciated in the past (with or without overtly religious language) may encourage them in what can be an uphill task. Occasionally it will be possible to go on from there and help them to think more creatively about the very notion of community: what it means for them and the group for which they are responsible; and how those who may be being squeezed out can be included.

**3.** A more specialist area of the same general concern is those who are trying to live in community. The new community movement is one of the great signs of hope in the Church and in society at large, and those who are taking that courageous and selfless step—for living in community is often very demanding—need all the support, from prayer to an encouraging smile, to a fat cheque, that we can give them. Perhaps most of all they need understanding friendship—and a bolt hole to which they can escape and regroup their moral and spiritual forces.

**4.** So far we have been thinking of strategies for the creation of community. Another whole area is the care of the victims of breakdowns in the community life of our society. That includes anyone who is made a victim of the concentrations and aggregations of power—from the old lady who is made anxious and fretful by an official form she doesn't understand, to those who fall foul of rules and authorities against which there is no appeal. Sometimes there may in theory be a right of appeal, as in planning applications, but the victims often lack the resources and the confidence to mount an appeal ... Then there are those who either do not wish to or are unable to cope with the bureaucratic hassle of securing a subsistence and so end up on the streets or in the hostels. They are the most poignant reminders of the failure of our community—even though they are sometimes so bruised as people that they positively do not want to be incorporated into anything recognisable as community.

**5.** Most of us live in neighbourhoods where there are in fact a number of points of entry into processes of participation—from the Parent Teachers' Association, to local government 'hearings' on plans for the neighbourhood, to shareholders' meetings, to open meetings of the local council. Equally, most of us have neither the time nor the energy nor the staying power to be regular and well-informed attenders at all of these. What is clear, though, is that authoritarianism and ultimately the destruction of community is bred less by malevolence than by apathy. We need to find the right balance between opting out entirely and becoming worn out busybodies as we rush from one forum to another. If we are members of a group, it can sometimes be helpful to divide the turf—but compare notes reasonably systematically, less on substance than on process. Three questions to put at the centre of that note-comparing are: who is really participating; and who is being kept out; and how?

**6.** On a wider canvas come the political processes in the general sense, from the local unit of elected government to the election of an MP and an MEP. There is so much that could be said under this head; I have to be highly selective and will restrict myself to three points. One, creating community in your locality need not be inconsistent with political involvement if you are unfailingly polite and considerate to those who disagree with your views. Two, whether or not you choose to be 'politically active' in the narrow sense, a key question to bear in mind constantly is not 'How can I make my viewpoint stick?' but 'How can we enlarge the circle amongst whom these issues are discussed?' Three, get into the habit of asking of any elected representative: 'For whom is he or she speaking?' and if the answer seems to be a narrow section of society, point that out to the representative involved, with an invitation to explain what is going on.

**7.** Finally, for your own information and as an exercise in grounding some of the material in this chapter, it might be helpful to find out who owns and controls (and that may not turn out to be the same thing) the local newspapers, magazines and radio stations in your area. You could then have a critical look at each and ask if the interests they represent are given improper weight in the media concerned. Does this constitute an abuse of power? If so, what can be done about it?

## APPRAISAL

Look over the whole process, from the reflection on the love of God to the most trivial action, and ask yourself where you have seen the values of the kingdom—in your inner life and in the outer life of your involvement. Where, too, at both levels have you seen those values most consistently denied? And can you think why?

The object is not to pass critical judgment; it is rather to discern what it is in you and in the groups in which you are involved that builds up community—and what it is that destroys it. Clearly you will want to encourage the former and prune the latter, though before you run amok with the shears, it is well to understand as much as you can about what it is that is getting in the way. It may well be an unhealed part of you; or, in an often surprisingly close analogy, an unhealed part of the community's life and memory.

That is why some wise counsellors and spiritual guides talk about 'the healing of memory', as applicable both to individuals and to communities. The healing can take the form of reliving the hurt or trauma, with everyone contributing their perspective to build up as complete a picture as possible, with the emphasis less on the factual consistency of the memories (it is rare and often suspicious if the memories dovetail perfectly) than on the emotional comprehensiveness of the memories. Have we got on the table all that everyone feels about that particular event? Different counsellors adopt different techniques from there on; one I like is simply inviting the Lord in to the memory of that event in the imagination, and reconstructing from the group's joint imaginative resources how he would react ... Naturally the process is helped if it is co-ordinated by someone who is 'outside' the event concerned.

Apart from pinpointing what might be emerging as obstacles to the process of community building, it is good to use the appraisal stage as a chance to check that the 'inner' and 'outer' parts of the cycle are integrating properly. To put it concretely, are you as an individual and are you as a group managing to pray effectively with (which is not quite the same as about) the experiences you are encountering in the action part of the cycle? And is the prayer leading and sustaining you in the action, or has the action acquired a dynamic of its own?

If you answer that last question in the affirmative, I suggest you pause and have a closer look at what is going on. To a degree, it is right that being involved in any of the areas that I have outlined in the last section will, as it were, propel you along. Action always develops its own inner logic (and if it doesn't seem to be doing so, that might be a sign that the action is not appropriate—or not yet appropriate). But there comes a point at which we begin to feel that there is something almost demonic in the pace at which the action pushes us. It is a subtle difference and one that requires much reflective wrestling to sort out. It was best described to me as the difference between being drawn and being driven. When it feels as if we are being driven, it is time to call a halt—even if it is only a temporary halt—while we ensure that the reflective and prayer components of the cycle are in place and functioning healthily.

A final caution: community creating and protecting, like community living, can be a bruising business. It sometimes feels as though men and women were designed to live in independent, self-contained units; or that 'participation' is a liberal witch-word better ignored. Quite. It is precisely because men and women have always preferred to run away from salvation that Moses was driven mad by people who wished they'd stayed in Egypt, and Jesus was sent to the cross. If you are running across the deep human desire for hell, you have much to irrigate in your prayer life—even if it makes you boil or freeze!

Chapter Four

# THE CULTURE OF VIOLENCE

## REFLECTION ON THE LOVE OF GOD

READ EXODUS 15:1–18

It was then that Moses and the sons of Israel sang this song in honour of Yahweh:

'Yahweh I sing: he has covered himself in glory,
horse and rider he has thrown into the sea.
Yah is my strength, my song,
he is my salvation.
This is my God, I praise him;
the God of my father, I extol him.
Yahweh is a warrior;
Yahweh is his name.
The chariots and the army of Pharaoh he has hurled into the sea;
the pick of his horsemen lie drowned in the Sea of Reeds.
The depths have closed over them;
they have sunk to the bottom like a stone.
Your right hand, Yahweh, shows majestic in power,
your right hand, Yahweh, shatters the enemy.
So great your splendour, you crush your foes;
you unleash your fury, and it devours them like stubble.
A blast from your nostrils and the waters piled high;
the waves stood upright like a dyke;
in the heart of the sea the deeps came together.

"I will give chase and overtake," the enemy said
"I shall share out the spoil, my soul will feast on it;
I shall draw my sword, my hand will destroy them."
One breath of yours you blew, and the sea closed over them;
they sank like lead in the terrible waters.
Who among the gods is your like, Yahweh?
Who is your like, majestic in holiness,
terrible in deeds of prowess, worker of wonders?
You stretched your right hand out, the earth swallowed them!
By your grace you led the people you redeemed,
by your strength you guided them to your holy house.
Hearing of this, the peoples tremble;
pangs seize on the inhabitants of Philistia.
Edom's chieftains are now dismayed,
the princes of Moab fall to trembling,
Canaan's inhabitants are all unmanned.
On them fall terror and dread;
through the power of your arm they are still as stone
as your people pass, Yahweh,
as the people pass whom you purchased.
You will bring them and plant them on the mountain that is your own,
the place you have made your dwelling, Yahweh,
the sanctuary, Yahweh, prepared by your own hands.
Yahweh will be king for ever and ever.'

This may seem a slightly perverse place to start a chapter on militarism. For here Yahweh is presented as the embodiment of the successful warrior (v.3). It is he who has set the people of Israel free and he has achieved that by a great military victory. There are three points that repay study.

First, we need to acknowledge that the Old Testament and, in parts, the New, seem to glorify military prowess. That such language can be read allegorically or symbolically is no doubt true, but that does not let us off the hook. For centuries Christian artists and poets (and for a much longer time Jewish artists and poets) have represented their God as one who delights in armed struggle, who works his purposes out on the battle field. We might begin therefore by acknowledging the part the Judaeo-Christian heritage has played, maybe unwittingly and through misinterpretation, in the maintenance of a militaristic culture.

Once faced, that can be put to one side. For while it is true that in the early stages of the religious consciousness of the Old Testament war is a means by which salvation is worked out, the reign of God is early seen as precluding violence. We get a glimpse of this in verses 17–18. The place for the people of God is the sanctuary, God's holy hill.

Third, notice how words like glory, majesty, grace and strength—which tend to be eviscerated in our liturgical use of them—have here a very direct and earthy reference. Yahweh's holiness is shown in his readiness to act in history to free his people. Here that historical activity takes the form of destruction. In the New Testament it will take the form of the cross. The tribal God who is worshipped in military victory is finally revealed as the cosmic God who is left to die nearly alone in disgrace and failure.

READ ISAIAH 2:2–5

In the days to come
the mountain of the Temple of Yahweh
shall tower above the mountains
and be lifted higher than the hills.
All the nations will stream to it,
peoples without number will come to it; and they will say:

'Come, let us go up to the mountain of Yahweh,
to the Temple of the God of Jacob
that he may teach us his ways
so that we may walk in his paths;
since the Law will go out from Zion,
and the oracle of Yahweh from Jerusalem.'

He will wield authority over the nations
and adjudicate between many peoples;
these will hammer their swords into ploughshares,
their spears into sickles.
Nation will not lift sword against nation,
there will be no more training for war.

O House of Jacob, come,
let us walk in the light of Yahweh.

We are once more at the holy hill, now identified as Jerusalem. The prophet looks forward to the day when 'the law' and 'the oracle' are shared by all the nations of the world. The implication is that when all humanity can live by the law of God, they will foreswear war and violence.

This passage is given particular piquancy by the fact that some scholars think that the 'oracle' is not a written code or part of the Mosaic law, but a person, a prophet who will live and proclaim that law so perfectly that the nations will be unable to resist him.

Here, then, there may be another pointer to the Christ-figure, the one who a later prophetic community in the same tradition was going to represent as the Suffering Servant. By understanding authority and power in terms of redemptive suffering, that Servant would go to the cross, and would found an ethic that has constantly put violence and the militaristic spirit under judgment.

READ MATTHEW 12:22–32

Then they brought to him a blind and dumb demoniac; and he cured him, so that the dumb man could speak and see. All the people were astounded and said, 'Can this be the Son of David?' But when the Pharisees heard this they said, 'The man casts out devils only through Beelzebul, the prince of devils.'

Knowing what was in their minds he said to them, 'Every kingdom divided against itself is heading for ruin; and no town, no household divided against itself can stand. Now if Satan casts out Satan, he is divided against himself; so how can his kingdom stand? And if it is through Beelzebul that I cast out devils, through whom do your own experts cast them out? Let them be your judges, then. But if it is through the Spirit of God that I cast devils out, then know that the kingdom of God has overtaken you.

'Or again, how can anyone make his way into a strong man's house and burgle his property unless he has tied up the strong man first? Only then can he burgle his house.

'He who is not with me is against me, and he who does not gather with me scatters. And so I tell you, every one of men's sins and blasphemies will be forgiven, but blasphemy against the Spirit will not be forgiven. And anyone who says a word against the Son of Man will be forgiven; but let anyone speak against the Holy Spirit and he will not be forgiven either in this world or in the next.'

It is important to read this story with an eye on the symbolism. The demoniac represents the forces of dis-integration, of violence, of irrationality, of breakdown. He cannot see: a symbol of a deeper blindness than mere sightlessness; he cannot speak, so he is beyond human contact. He can be taken as the archetypal figure of all that renders human community impossible. Yet Jesus cures him—and thereby introduces a discussion about the ultimate power of the forces of evil. The central fact is that Jesus is greater than those powers, and his mission and ministry are precisely to rid the world of their domination (v.28).

To fail to recognise that or to try to compromise the work of the Spirit in proclaiming that the reign of God has started is thus the final blasphemy.

It is wholly consistent with the Old Testament message that the proclamation of the time that the prophets longed to see is marked by conflict and misunderstanding. The Son of God is confused with the prince of darkness, and those who should have been shouting hosannas are surlily plotting his downfall. Caught in their own certainties and false securities, they are incapable of recognising the moment of grace.

READ JOHN 20:19–26

In the evening of that same day, the first day of the week, the doors were closed in the room where the disciples were, for fear of the Jews. Jesus came and stood among them. He said to them, 'Peace be with you', and showed them his hands and his side. The disciples were filled with joy when they saw the Lord, and he said to them again, 'Peace be with you.

'As the Father sent me,
so am I sending you.'

After saying this he breathed on them and said:

'Receive the Holy Spirit.
For those whose sins you forgive,
they are forgiven;
for those whose sins you retain,
they are retained.'

Thomas, called the Twin, who was one of the Twelve, was not with them when Jesus came. When the disciples said, 'We have seen the Lord', he answered, 'Unless I see the holes that the nails made in his hands and can put my finger into the holes they made, and unless l can put my hand into his side, I refuse to believe.' Eight days later the disciples were in the house again and Thomas was with them. The doors were closed, but Jesus came in and stood among them. 'Peace be with you,' he said.

The contrast with the resurrected Christ is striking. The victory over the forces of evil has objectively been won. Thus the risen Christ can greet his friends with the conventional Jewish greeting 'Peace be with you'—but a convention that has been revolutionised by the events of the last three days. (The repetition of the greeting can be taken to indicate that the Evangelist wants us to see in it something more than the conventions of Jewish good manners.)

The peace which the risen Christ proclaims as a fact is not just absence of conflict. It is essentially the assurance that all the powers of disintegration, symbolised heretofore by the blind and dumb demoniac, have been conquered so that there are now no constraints on the human spirit's progress towards union with Father, Son and Holy Spirit.

And what is true of the individual is true of the wider communities of societies and nations. The moment that the prophet Isaiah longed for is here—but it is here only in anticipation, in potential. Men and women have to learn to live it out, to accomplish it as fact ... We are still, heaven help us, learning.

READ EPHESIANS 2:11–22

Do not forget, then, that there was a time when you who were pagans physically, termed the Uncircumcised by those who speak of themselves as the Circumcision by reason of a physical operation, do not forget, I say, that you had no Christ and were excluded from membership of Israel, aliens with no part in the covenants with their Promise; you were immersed in this world, without hope and without God. But now in Christ Jesus, you that used to be so far apart from us have been brought very close, by the blood of Christ. For he is the peace between us, and has made the two into one and broken down the barrier which used to keep them apart, actually destroying in his own person the hostility caused by the rules and decrees of the Law. This was to create one single New Man in himself out of the two of them and by restoring peace through the cross, to unite them both in a single Body and reconcile them with God. In his own person he killed the hostility. Later he came to bring the good news of peace, peace to you who were far away and peace to those who were near at hand. Through him, both of us have in the one Spirit our way to come to the Father.

So you are no longer aliens or foreign visitors: you are citizens like all the saints, and part of God's household. You are part of a building that has the apostles and prophets for its foundations, and Christ Jesus himself for its main cornerstone. As every structure is aligned on him, all grow into one holy temple in the Lord; and you too, in him, are being built into a house where God lives, in the Spirit.

This is one of the great passages of Christian faith—that Christ has broken down the walls of division between the chosen people and the rest of humanity. Now it makes sense to dream of a new creation—one in which the peace and harmony promised by the prophets can in fact be achieved. But the centre of that, its guarantor, is Christ. It is he who has swept away the old divisions and opened up the prospect of the universal salvation of the whole of humanity.

We need to get this right. We are not here offered an assurance that the vision that, for example, motivated the founders of the United Nations can be met by our politicians. The language of the epistle is intensely religious, rather than political or social. The prospect of unity and harmony that it offers is rooted and grounded in the person and story of Jesus Christ. 'Through him, both of us have in the one Spirit our way to come to the Father.' That is the issue. But it is implied that as we come to the Father, so we come to each other. The joyful journey of discovery of our common Father is—and for the Christian always has to be—prior.

READ 1 JOHN 4:15–21

If anyone acknowledges that Jesus is the Son of God,
God lives in him, and he in God.
We ourselves have known and put our faith in
God's love towards ourselves.
God is love
and anyone who lives in love lives in God,
and God lives in him.
Love will come to its perfection in us
when we can face the day of Judgement without fear;
because even in this world
we have become as he is.
In love there can be no fear,
but fear is driven out by perfect love:
because to fear is to expect punishment,
and anyone who is afraid is still imperfect in love.
We are to love, then,
because he loved us first.
Anyone who says, 'I love God',
and hates his brother,
is a liar,

since a man who does not love the
brother that he can see
cannot love God, whom he has never
seen.

So this is the commandment that he
has given us,
that anyone who loves God must also
love his brother.

In a passage that can be read at several levels, John links the acceptance of Jesus as the Christ—something that his contemporaries found so difficult, as we have already seen—with the indwelling of God and therefore the final claim of the ethic of love. That claim is absolute, not in the sense that love is absolute but in the sense that we can bar absolutely no one from the offer of life.

The political and social implications of this claim are far-reaching. For they lead us to refuse to accept the state of enmity or hostility as final or natural or acceptable. 'We are to love because'—not because they are loveable or because they will return our love or because loving them will be good for us—but 'because he loved us first'.

How far we have travelled from the first reading! The great Yahweh who declares himself in wholesale slaughter of (in some senses at least) innocent Egyptian soldiers is a God whose only claim upon us is that of love—and whose only demand upon us is that of love ... But that is a demand he presses so urgently that we shall need to consider very carefully what it means for the way we conceive of defence, of 'threats to our security', of the values that underlie so much of our individual thinking and collective action in this deeply debated area.

## ANALYSIS

In no area of North Atlantic life is there more general disquiet than in that of defence and the threat of nuclear annihilation. From psychological studies of children's dreams and fantasies to the ratings of TV documentaries on the effects of nuclear war, the evidence is overwhelming: the north Atlantic community knows at the visceral level that nuclear destruction presents a judgment on its values and its politics that is quite literally critical.

Even in the southern hemisphere where it might be thought the nuclear threat is less obvious, the politics of nuclear disarmament have been a major feature of New Zealand's political life for ten years; a major feature of political, medical and even genetic life in Micronesia for twenty years as a result of French nuclear testing; and a discernible if less dramatic theme in Australian politics and public discussion since the strategic importance of American facilities in northern Australia brought home to the Australian public that in a nuclear war there is no neutrality and no safe hiding place.

What is unique about the nuclear threat is its immediacy. The world may choke in its own polluted juices if it neglects the kairos of the environment. Tens of millions of people may lead degraded and foreshortened lives if the world neglects the kairos of mass poverty. If it fumbles the nuclear issue, the world will be destroyed. The attempts to calculate how many people would survive a nuclear war are as irrelevant as they are ill-conceived. Life would be unlivable in the most seriously affected areas which, in the case of a full-scale confrontation between the super powers, we would have to assume would be the majority of the land mass of Europe and North America. Elsewhere the resultant atmospheric pollution would have incalculable climatic and genetic effects.

People are right to be frightened, not least because of the unpredictability and the potentially fatal consequences of human error. It is known, for example, that on at least three occasions in the West human error has led to full scale alerts which could have resulted in the 'accidental' launching of nuclear missiles. On the Soviet side, human fallibility was exposed at Chernobyl: there is little reason to assume that military personnel are less fallible than civilian nuclear engineers. Indeed, there are some reasons for thinking they may be more fallible.

Christians bring a particular perspective to this issue. Believing that God created the world and saw that it was good, and that Christ died for it, we do not view its destruction merely as a threat to our own generation. While a kind of historical relativity may be in order when we contemplate the passing of our particular civilisation, it is quite another matter when we consider the wilful destruction of incalculable numbers of people and areas of land in a nuclear holocaust. Whatever the moral deserts of our nations, no Christian can contemplate the use of nuclear weapons—notwithstanding the precedents of Hiroshima and Nagasaki—with anything but abhorrence.

It is therefore no surprise that much Christian energy currently goes into protesting against the development and deployment of nuclear weaponry. In every country of the free world, Christians have played a significant and in many cases a leading role in calling for nuclear disarmament—whether multilateral, unilateral, conditional, unconditional, immediate or phased. It is not my purpose in this chapter to enter the debates that such advocacy has produced. The literature is extensive and readily available. It is,

Holy War. Volunteers march in Teheran before being sent to the front in the war with Iraq.

however, my intention to argue that the kairos to which Christians are called to be alert is indeed indicated by the nuclear threat. But it is much more extensive than that threat alone. The nuclear threat is a finger pointing at something much more sinister.

The horror and immediacy of nuclear holocaust have foreshortened horizons. The nuclear threat has a dual nature. First, it is the tip of an iceberg, the presenting symptom of a much wider and deeper malaise. Second, its very horror serves to deflect the forces that sustain it into new forms. On the one hand, it embodies as its epitome cultural violence. On the other, it ensures that while the ultimate violence remains as threat, the reality of violence is re-enacted in proxy wars, in international terrorism, in civil war, in a whole sub-set of military and paramilitary adventures. Sustained by the political and economic support of the super powers, in whose hands lie the possibility of ultimate nuclear disaster, these 'lesser' conflicts none the less exact, directly and indirectly, a toll that bears comparison with that of a nuclear exchange.

Seen from this perspective, the Christian is called not merely to campaign for nuclear disarmament but to campaign against what lies behind nuclear armament, namely, the culture of militarism and violence. For it is this culture that fuels nuclear weaponry—but also 'conventional' weapons, military systems, chemical and biological warfare, the militarisation of space, internal repression, torture, and the belief that force is an acceptable way of solving social conflicts.

The kairos with which we are presented, then, arises from the fact that the nuclear threat forces us back to see the culture of militarism from the perspective of the gospel of God. It obliges us to recognise that the culture of militarism, and associated with it the culture of violence, has become one of the dominant components of our social, political, economic and intellectual life. It is one of the great ironies of history that nations which publicly pose as defenders of Christian civilisation simultaneously incorporate an ideology, a way of looking at things, which Jesus explicitly foreswore.

Where, then, does this culture come from? How does it manifest itself? How is it sustained? What are its effects? These are questions that we shall have to consider one by one.

## 1. THE ORIGINS OF THE CULTURE OF MILITARISM

Different disciplines offer a variety of starting points. Psychologists, for instance, point to a distorted idea of maleness. They see a corrupted male principle as making inevitable that glorification of force which is the essence of the culture of militarism. The male lust to penetrate and dominate becomes distorted when it is cut off from the balancing female principles of accommodation, conciliation and acceptance. On this view, then, a misconceived notion of what it is to be male becomes an important, perhaps even a fundamental, power behind the culture of militarism.

Certainly if one examines the cultures of highly militarised regimes, for example, Nazi Germany, contemporary South Africa, or pre-Falklands Argentina, the relationship between militarism and a particular interpretation (a particularly misformed interpretation) of maleness, manliness is very apparent. The goose-step and the Nazi salute may be good symbols of that relationship.

Furthermore, this misinterpretation of maleness (typically disseminated by Hollywood) generates slogans of 'walking tall'. The reference is to the righteous Frontiers Man, the white-hatted cowboy of Hollywood imagery, who fears nothing because he is quicker on the draw and shoots straighter than anyone in town. 'Walking tall' is translated into international politics in much the same terms. As a political idea, it draws from literary, cinematic and historical sources to express a particular concept of masculinity, in which morality and ethics may be, at least, ambivalent. For every *High Noon*, there is a Sundance Kid.

Historians, too, have much to contribute to our understanding of the origins of the culture of militarism. They point out that you cannot understand present distributions of wealth and political power, both nationally and internationally, without recognising the fundamental role played by military superiority throughout history. In the end, empire has always depended on military superiority; in the end, systems of conciliation and negotiation have historically been swept aside, and issues have been settled—in some sense at least—by force of arms. It is simply false to imagine that the world is not vitally shaped by relative superiority in the power to kill.

Secure in this conviction, history plays its own part in replicating the culture of militarism. Although there are signs of change, for over 2,000 years the stuff of history has been the record of military prowess. Children and nations have been brought up to believe that battles and wars and military heroes, conquests, invasions, sieges and campaigns constitute 'the history' of a people. If historians believe that history is determined by military superiority, history inevitably comes to be represented as the record of that superiority.

Sociologists, too, have much to contribute to the understanding of the origins of the culture of militarism. They invite us to look at the role played by the military in any society. Whether in so-called primitive societies or in contemporary Russia and America, military accomplishment is a source of rank, prestige, power and social acceptance. Further, what is true for individuals is true for institutions. Military and paramilitary organisations—the Pentagon, the CIA, the Ministry of Defence, MI5, MI6—acquire a degree of social power quite independent of elected authority, and in some cases use their power to subvert that authority.

If, then, you ask where prestige, influence and power in any society reside, in nearly every society part of the answer will lie in 'the military'. That will not be the whole answer. In a more open and democratic society, it may be less adequate as a total answer, but in very few societies indeed can it be ignored altogether.

The list could go on. Linguistic studies remind us how much of our language has a military origin. We talk of fighting a battle, for example, against inflation or promiscuity. We talk of winning victories—in sport and politics. We talk of ammunition, of fire power, of being in command, of siege, defeat and rout. Our language is studded with military references; so too, of course, are our literature, our art, our films, and even our music. How odd a peaceable Martian would find it that one of our greatest and most revered musical masterpieces is punctuated by cannon fire. How odd he would find it that the two most successful genres of films are war and westerns. Indeed, one needn't appeal to Martians: a young New Zealander visiting London for the first time remarked to me: 'What warlike people you are. Wherever I go, I see generals on horseback, admirals on columns, standards draped in churches, magnificent tombs and monuments to the successful butchers of innocent and uncomprehending people. What a relief it was to find Poets' Corner. But what a commentary on you Brits, that you allow your poets only a corner.'

## 2. THE MAINTENANCE OF THE CULTURE OF MILITARISM

Since General Eisenhower complained of the power of 'the military-industrial complex', social scientists have become increasingly interested in the relationship between the military and its suppliers. Without in any way underestimating the contribution of the maintenance of the culture of militarism made by language, films, history or psychology, there is reason to give the major role in the West to the symbiotic relation that has developed between military consumers and industrial producers. The most obvious example is in scientific research. It is estimated that worldwide one in four scientists works directly on military projects. Between 1977 and 1985 global expenditure in real terms on military

The SDI (Strategic Defence Initiative) was announced by President Reagan in 1983. Its intention is to use laser and particle-beam technology to attack enemy missiles from earth orbit. In 1987, the USSR admitted that it was carrying out research into similar weapons systems.

research and development increased by 85 per cent. Military research was a growth industry indeed.

In this sense the scientific establishment is as dependent on the military for its funding, its livelihood, its prestige as are defence contractors. But to put it like that is a gross over-simplification, not least because it represents the defence contractors as the passive recipients of orders from the military. In fact, the defence industry as a whole, including many large firms such as Plessey, Ferranti, Racal, and GEC, which produce for both military and non-military markets, ensure that their relationship with the military is much more interactive.

This proactive relationship has reached its fullest expression in the United States where the defence contractors have ensured that not a single Congressman can speak against military expenditure without risking substantial protest from a significant employer in his own constituency. By ensuring that protests against increased military expenditure cost votes, the defence industry in the United States acts as a prime protector of military expenditure. It has, of course, a powerful ally among the military planners and bureaucrats for whom larger budgets mean larger staffs, greater prestige and more rapid promotion.

Some commentators have argued that there is an even more subtle and invidious relationship between the military industrial complex and the culture of militarism. They argue that it is not only large firms that have a stake in military expenditure and therefore protect it from radical reform by elected legislators. A parallel relationship, they argue, lies between the defence establishment as a whole and the way in which news and analysis is presented to the public in North America and Europe. The least objectionable aspect of this relationship is the activity of security analysts and commentators, many of whom flit between academic, media, political and military or quasi-military bases. Thus people like Breszinski, Schlesinger and Kissinger in the United States, and the current Director of the Royal Institute for International Affairs in the UK rationalise and make legitimate the culture of militarism, presenting it as 'hard-headed', 'realistic', 'sensible', 'politically attractive', and even 'inevitable' through media such as serious journals, heavyweight newspapers and TV programmes. These, we are told, are the people 'who know'. They have the experience, knowledge and political antennae denied the rest of us. Thus Sir Ronald Mason, who from 1977–1983 was the Chief Scientific Advisor of the British Ministry of Defence, and then, notice, Deputy Chairman of Hunting Engineering, was able to dismiss Professor E. P. Thompson's critical book on the strategic defence initiative as 'extravagant nonsense'.

More subtle because less visible is the relationship between the military industrial complex and the way in which news is covered, presented and slanted. The crass forms of this kind of manipulation that led the CIA to fund *Encounter* magazine in the 1960s has given way to something much more subtle. It is more delicate than Conservative Party fury over the BBC coverage of the Falklands War and the bombing of Libya. It has more to do with the barely visible links between the way news is presented and the interests of the military industrial complex. These are varied in form, running from advertising revenue, the presentation of information, ownership of financial stakes in news media, and the interests of the state as mediated through regulation of news media and, particularly, broadcasting. The purge of senior management in the BBC in 1986/87 is only one example; the fiasco over *Spycatcher* another. This is not to impugn the honesty or impartiality of editors or television producers. As Robin Luckham has put it: 'There are degrees of impartiality, yet the debate about defence takes place within a subtly shaped consensus that is not easily discerned.' The military industrial complex and its acolytes and dependents play a central role, so it is argued, in the shaping of that consensus.

## 3. DEMONSTRATIONS OF THE CULTURE OF MILITARISM

As one would expect, the culture of militarism expresses itself in many ways. We shall here be concerned not with its artistic expression—important though that is for its maintenance—but rather its political expression, since it is that which ultimately costs people their life.

The first political expression is in the *ideology of national security*, that is, the system of ideas and policies that puts national security at the centre of political activity and defines it in terms of the protection of status, wealth and power by military and paramilitary methods. Internal and external threats to those existing distributions are thus met with a military response. Indeed, it is typical of states in which national security ideology has become deeply entrenched that military personnel are used for internal repression. They thus acquire political influence and, often, direct power, typically by a military coup as in South Korea in 1980 or, very nearly, the Philippines in 1987.

The ideology of national security has often proved attractive to the Church.

Because the ideology represents threats to existing distributions as 'communist', 'unchristian', 'alien' or 'subversive', the Church has often aligned itself with the champions of national security, irrespective of both their means and their ends. It has in this way become the chaplain of the culture of militarism. Although of course there are nearly always dissident voices, even within the denomination most closely allied with the ideal of national security—for example, the Roman Catholic Church in Chile, or the Presbyterian Church in South Korea—the Church plays a part in maintaining the culture of militarism precisely at the point at which it ought to be challenging it most trenchantly.

This takes us to a second demonstration of the culture of militarism, and one which is even more disturbing to the Christian conscience: *the Crusade or Holy War*. This has, of course, a long history in both Christianity and Islam. (Though interestingly not in Buddhism or Hinduism.) It is tempting for Christians to imagine that the rise of Islamic fundamentalism and with it the rediscovery of the Jihad—a rediscovery that has brought not only violence to the Middle East but international terrorism to many countries of Europe—is the only example of the direct coalition of religious interests and the culture of militarism. We too easily forget not only Northern Ireland but the 'regular' wars such as the Falklands War and the Vietnam War, where religious leadership was mobilised to declare that the cause was God's cause, and that therefore he would deliver victory. If the Church has too easily been duped into supporting the culture of militarism in its internal aspects in national security states, it has been hardly less easily duped into supporting its external expressions by giving them some of the elements of the Crusades.

The full significance of that becomes apparent when we consider the third manifestation of the culture of militarism, namely its ideological expressions, and slogans: *might is right*. It is implied in both national security ideology and in the Crusades that military might is self-justifying. He who wins proves his point. Victory settles arguments because the vanquished cannot argue. This of course is the very antithesis of law, ethics or morality. For at its crudest, the self-interest (even the ethical self-interest) of the strongest judges itself superior to the ethics of the weakest purely on the grounds of its own strength. 'Walking tall' thus becomes an end in itself, and there is a point at which questions about the purpose of walking tall, the ethics maintained by walking tall, become impossible.

Slogans, of course, may well be engineered: the defence of freedom; peace through strength; security through military superiority, are all examples of such slogans. They can only remain slogans, for the culture of militarism assumes that its military

The Middle East has been an arms dealer's paradise since the 1960s. The result has been a ready supply of weapons ranging from tanks and aircraft through to the guns used on the streets of Beirut.

power *is* freedom. It *is* peace.

It is no surprise to find that in May Day in Moscow; in the Royal Tournament in London; in passing-out parades in St Cyr; and in the great displays of military power that take place in South Africa, rhetoric, slogans, and symbols combine to bring together crude military power, nationalism, and basic political values (for example, the socialist revolution in Russia, the maintenance of white superiority in South Africa). Alternative ideologies, alternative definitions of and strategies for security, cease to be permissible; ethics come out of the barrel of a gun.

We turn now from the relatively abstract to the brutally concrete. For the fourth form of the culture of militarism, already implied in the last paragraph, is the *worship of the weapon*. It is out of the worship of the weapon that the arms trade grows, for he who has the most potent weapon has the best chance of being proved right. That basic observation of real-politik generates not only the arms race in the sense in which that phrase is usually understood in the North Atlantic but also the competitive weapon worship between countries that either can't afford arms at all, such as India, Bangladesh and Pakistan, or in which the level of international tension makes the ownership of arms—better and better

Iranian soldiers in combat against Iraqi troops. The war between Iran and Iraq flared in 1980, and has since claimed hundreds of thousands of lives.

arms at that—a treadmill. In the heyday of OPEC, the Middle East was flooded with arms salesmen from all the major arms exporting countries, not excluding the Soviet Union. The crisis in the Gulf in 1987 arose directly from the arms race that then ensued.

It is no surprise to discover that it is in America that worship of the weapon reaches its apogee. At the individual level it is ritualised in the resistance to gun control. At the national level it achieves its ultimate expression in the so-called Strategic Defence Initiative, SDI or 'Starwars'.

SDI represents an attempt to produce the ultimate weapon. According to President Reagan, SDI was to be the weapon system that rendered nuclear weapons obsolete. Although it was presented to the American public and later the European public as an entirely defensive system, it is in reality essentially offensive, giving America what she has always, if inconsistently, craved—clear strategic superiority. However far out the technology and however incalculable the human system interface (requiring the gravest strategic and political decisions to be made within seconds), SDI takes worship of the weapon to its ultimate conclusion. No wonder President Reagan was reluctant to abandon it at Reykjavik, in Washington and, in 1988, in Moscow. It is too powerful a symbol for a leader who knows very well how to manipulate the symbols of his culture.

That brings us to the last expression of the culture of militarism. Again, it has been implied in the foregoing paragraphs but it now needs to be spelt out explicitly. The culture of militarism leads inevitably to the assertion that *security rests in military might*. I am safe only if I have more fire power than any conceivable opponent. Such a proposition runs immediately into conflict with the logic of western defence analysts. That logic assumes that security comes from parity, especially if that parity of weaponry delivers what Robert Macnamara called mutually assured destruction. Parity of arms and mutually assured destruction together provide the strongest disincentive to the use of nuclear weapons, and therefore ensure such peace as the Super Powers have enjoyed since 1945.

The culture of militarism, however, cannot quite settle for parity. It strives always for sufficient superiority to ensure victory in the event of war. The struggle between parity and superiority has thus been the key in the history of strategic planning and the irreconcilable contradiction in disarmament negotiations for the last twenty years. That contradiction constantly surfaces in the US administration, sending inconsistent, contradictory and destabilising messages to the Russians, as preparations for Rekjavik and the Stockholm Conference showed. It is by no means impossible that it exists on the Russian side, too, with obvious implications for the conduct of arms control negotiations.

The real logic of mutually assured destruction does not even require parity: it requires merely the capacity to 'destroy' the enemy. One tenth of the nuclear arsenal of the United States, Britain and France would be more than enough to ensure that. The demand for parity comes more from certain naive politics, what Mary Kaldor has called the 'baroque arsenal', than from strategic logic. In a way it represents a compromise between the logic of mutually assured destruction and the logic of the culture of militarism. For the former could sanction enormous unilateral reductions in the nuclear arsenal of the western world, while the latter will constantly demand qualitative and quantitative improvements in an attempt to overhaul the enemy. A graphic illustration came in 1987/88. The super powers signed a historic arms reduction treaty in 1987; less than three months later, NATO increased its deployment of nuclear missiles to more than offset (by a factor of two) the reduction in US arms.

The superiority that the culture of militarism seeks is not confined to technical or numerical superiority in arms alone. It includes and indeed finds important expression in strategic and territorial superiority. This is best illustrated with respect to two areas: Central America and Afghanistan. In 1963 the USSR sought to establish territorial superiority by building missile bases in Cuba within a few minutes' flying time of the US coastline. Strategically this was relatively unimportant since one must assume that Russian submarines patrolled the US seaboard twenty-four hours a day. None the less, the symbolic power of such bases was enormous—to both Russia and to the United States. In much the same way, strategists in the Pentagon currently fear that Russia will be able to launch missiles from Nicaragua or, in the event of a left-inclined revolution in El Salvador, from that country. Again, the strategic issues are unimportant and the symbolic issues are all important. Convinced that the Sandinistas will sooner or later give the Russians rights to bases in Nicaragua, President Reagan's obsession stoops to direct and blatant breaches of international law to overthrow them. He, and it seems a majority of Americans, play high stakes for a symbol.

In Afghanistan the details were very different, but the essential issue was the same. Russia wished to deny to the West the territorial superiority that would be implied by a westward leaning government in Kabul. Russia's problem in Afghanistan was almost identical to that of the United States in Nicaragua: it could find no way out which would leave its basic objectives secure. Ultimately it had, it seems, to abandon these objectives. Hence the culture of militarism puts both super powers in absurd but insoluble positions. We are in a world where Beckett and Ionesco suddenly seem reasonable.

For it is out of this logic that proxy wars are born—thirty-six of them in 1986 alone. Wherever war or the threat of war breaks out, the super powers fear that the opposite side will emerge with some kind of territorial and/or political advantage, an advantage which they may be able to use either in a global strategic sense, for example, by threatening sea lanes, or in a diplomatic sense by showing that they protect their friends and/or defeat their friends' enemies. In either case, the need is to deprive the other side of superiority and ideally acquire it for oneself. For it is in the acquisition of that superiority—whether territorial, political or diplomatic—that security resides. Thus, in a peculiar inversion of logic, the commitment of resources and even personnel to wars in the Horn of Africa, in the Gulf of Arabia, in Mozambique, in Namibia, and supremely in Israel and the Middle East, is made in the name of security. The culture of militarism has become the cult of militarism, with an insatiable demand for human sacrifice.

## WHAT CAN BE DONE?

Like Moloch, the cult of militarism demands a constant supply of human blood. There have been over 300 wars since 1945: in that time, there has been no single day free of war somewhere in the world. But that is only the most obvious form of the sacrifice raised to its most frightful form in the Iraq/Iran war by the use of gas by one side and 'human wave' tactics by the other.

Barely less affected are the people in the First World, the Second World and the Third World, who are deprived of better life chances by the massive diversion of resources to arms and the military machine that is demanded by the cult of militarism. For example, the World Health Organisation spent around $83 million over ten years to eradicate smallpox. That amount is less than two hours' worth of global military expenditure. Similarly, to eradicate malaria—the killer disease that claims the lives of over a million children every year—requires twelve hours' worth of global military expenditure. To provide adequate housing for all the world's population according to locally acceptable standards would take about two weeks' worth of military expenditure. The economic prospects of many developing countries, from Turkey to Bangladesh, from Pakistan to Ethiopia, would be transformed if the excessive expenditures of both domestic currency and foreign currency on the military machine in these low income countries could

The frequent parading of military hardware in Moscow has all the trappings of worship—worship of the state and of military might.

1917

The devastation of Hiroshima by one atomic bomb, on 6 August 1945, killed 100,000 men, women and children. Hiroshima has become symbolic in the atomic age of the fear and dread of a final, ultimate use of nuclear weapons.

## MAJOR CONFLICTS AROUND THE WORLD

from 1945 to 1984.

1945
Partition of Germany

1920–48
Palestine Mandate

1943–9
Greek Civil War

1945–6
Vietnam

1945–9
Chinese Civil War

1945–54
Philippines revolt

1946
Punjab

1946–56
Indo-China

1947
Madagascar—revolt

1947–9
Kashmir

1947
Paraguay—Civil War

1948
Costa Rica—Civil War

1948–9
Arab-Israeli War

1953
Laos—Civil War

1954
Guatemala invaded

1955–9
Cyprus

1955–9
Jabel Akhdar War

1955–72
Sudan—Civil War

1956
Polish uprising

1956
Hungarian uprising

1956–7
Suez War

1956–61
Cuba

1957
Ifri Incident

1957
Honduras/Nicaragua

1957–9
Oman

1957–75
Vietnam

1958
Quemoy, Matsu, Taiwan

1958–83
Lebanon

1959
Cuban revolt

1960–71
Congo Civil War

1961
Bizerta Crisis

1961–75
Angola

1961–79
Kurdistan

1962
Sino-Indian Dispute

1962–6
Indonesia

1962–9
Yemen Civil War

1963+
Cyprus

1963+
Aden

1966–70
Nigerian Civil War

1967
The Six Day War

1968
Russians invade Czechoslovakia

1969+
Northern Ireland

1970
Jordan—Civil War

1970+
Cambodia/Kampuchea

1970s
Eritrea

1971
Bangladesh

1971+
Uganda

1972
Cod War

1973
Yom Kippur War

1974–82
Sinai

1975
North & South Vietnam

1979+
Nicaragua

1980
El Salvador

Early 1980s
Rhodesia Zimbabwe

1980+
Gulf War

1982
PLO Diaspora

1982
Falklands War

1983
US invade Grenada

Some conflicts have occurred over indeterminate periods...

Portuguese Guinea

Mozambique

Namibia

Somalia/Ogaden

Nepal—Civil Wars

Sino-Soviet disputes

S. America—Civil Wars

1948–58
Burma—
Civil Wars

1948–60
Malayan Emergency

1949
Thailand

1949
Algeria

1950–1
Chinese occupy Tibet

1950–3
Korean War

1950–61
Indonesian Civil War

1952–60
Kenya

1963+
Chad—
Civil War

1964
Radfan

1965
Indo-
Pakistan War

1965–6
Indonesia—massacres

1965–75
War in Dhofar

1976
Western Sahara

1979
Chinese invade Vietnam

1979
Russians invade Afghanistan

be diverted to supplying education, health care, housing and jobs to the people who currently lack them.

The trends are not auspicious, except perhaps in Africa where the decline in arms imports reflects the economic crisis that has afflicted that continent since the mid-seventies. If we look at the figures in more detail, the impact of declining oil prices in Nigeria, Gabon, Libya and Algeria is clear. More sombre is the evidence of *rising* arms expenditures in the rest of Africa, reflecting the level of tension associated with the conflict with South Africa. Thus Zimbabwe, a country with great developmental and reconstruction needs, spends a higher proportion of its national income on defence than the UK—and the UK is one of the world's big spenders, with the highest expenditure per head of the population in Europe ($521 in 1983–1985).

But as the sharts on page 140 show, it is the Middle East where arms sales have grown most dramatically, so that the region now accounts for nearly half of all Third World imports of arms. Although Saudi Arabia is the largest single importer, the rate of growth in other countries has been even faster.

In this context, the effect of the Iran/Iraq war has been shattering. The Swedish International Peace Research Institute has estimated that in 1985 Iraq was spending 57 per cent of its national

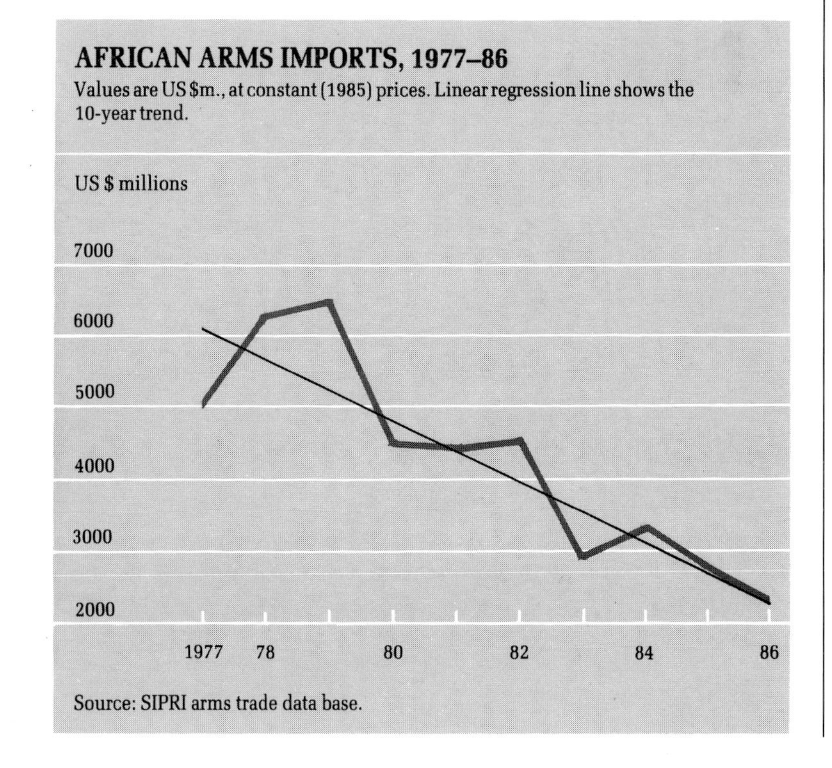

## THIRD WORLD IMPORTS OF MAJOR WEAPONS, BY REGION, 1967–86

Based on SIPRI trend indicator values, as expressed in US $m., at constant (1985) prices; 5-year moving averages.

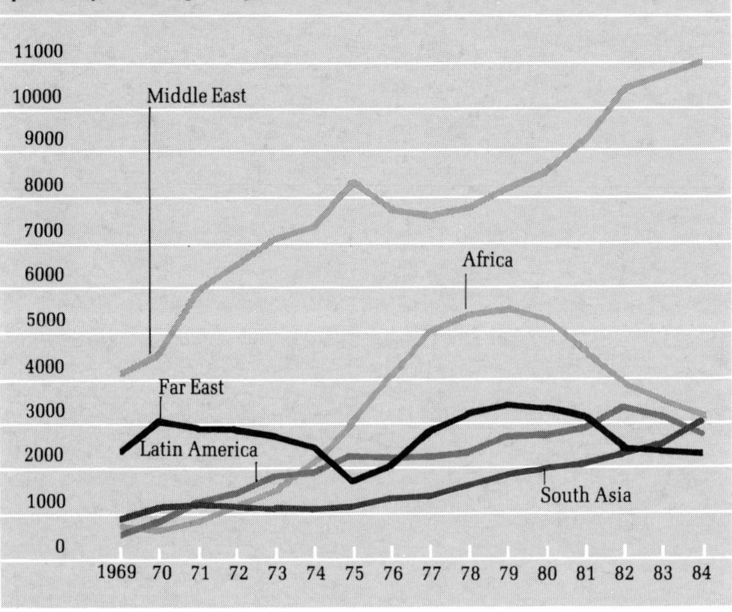


## THIRD WORLD IMPORTS OF MAJOR WEAPONS, BY REGION, 1982–86

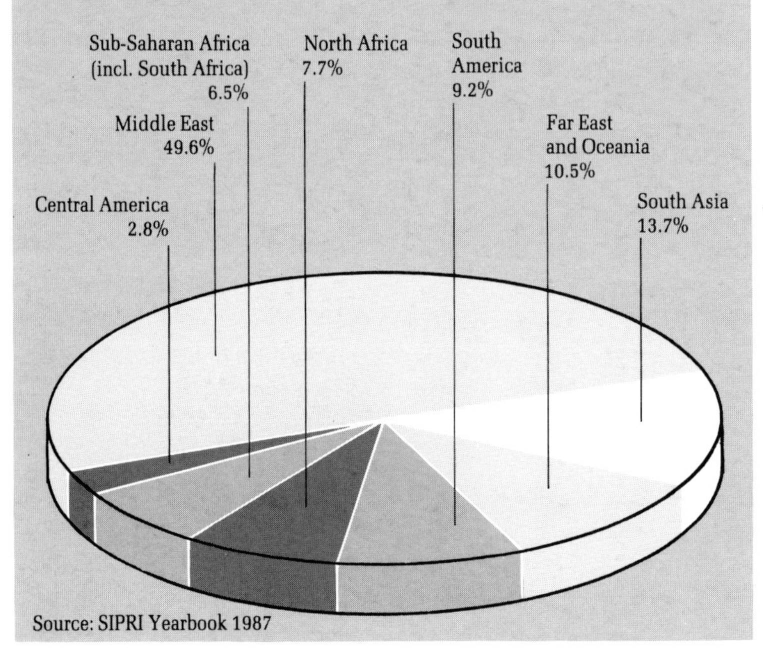


Source: SIPRI Yearbook 1987

income on the military. The figures for Iran are uncertain, but may approach the same level.

More surprising is the source of arms for this conflict.

Many Third World countries are involved in both supplying and importing arms. This raises a wider issue—the growth of the Third World as arms suppliers. Four countries are now so sophisticated that they are regular suppliers to industrialised nations; but for all Third World suppliers, the Middle and Far East remain the major markets.

It is, however, too easy to criticise the Third World for buying and selling arms. The basic point, that arms cost hospitals, schools, libraries and leisure, is no less true in the developed world.

By cutting military expenditure (and avoiding being drawn into an SDI race), the USSR could bring about the dramatic shift from an austerity economy to a mass consumption economy which it has long been postponing in order to make resources available for its military forces. Perhaps in the end nothing would contribute so much to international peace and harmony than that transformation. Sir Alec Douglas Home, as he then was, may not have been so wide of the mark when, justifying trade with Russia, he said that a fat communist was less of a threat than a hungry one. Transposed into slightly less homely imagery, it may well be true that a communist regime that could genuinely deliver a high standard of living to its people would the more quickly forget or neglect the supposed international mission of communism. By the same token, if the US and UK could be persuaded to spend on arms no more than the European average (as a proportion of national income) resources would be available—at least in theory—to deal with the homelessness and social deprivation that currently afflict both big spenders.

There are, then, high stakes to play for.

How are we to proceed?

We recognise at once a feeling that will not be new to readers of this book: a sense of helplessness and powerlessness. How, we ask ourselves, are we able to transform a culture that is so deeply rooted in our history, our literature, our politics, our economics, our very ways of thinking and being? That is always the question of the kairos.

The kairos, however, is not the moment of power, of control; it is not even the moment of certainty. It is the moment of weakness, of powerlessness, of failure and inability. It is kairos not because men and women are ready, able and in control but because God is willing.

The cost of military expenditures is felt most keenly by those whose real needs go unmet because resources are pre-empted by the military.

DAVE

## PRAYER

Prayer for peace and non-violence is above all prayer for the transformation of the spirit of militarism. It is therefore part of the prayer for the coming of the kingdom of God, in which the graces of gentleness, generosity and forgiveness make possible a quality of human and social relationship founded on love.

That is an ambitious prayer. And like all ambitious prayer it demands that we start with an acknowledgement of all the violence and ungentleness in our own lives. It is only when we can see that and ask to be freed from it that we can rightly dispose ourselves for prayer for the world.

Again, it is important to get the nuance right. I am not urging you to self-flagellation and a permanent life in the sewers of guilt. Not at all. Perhaps because I am so aware of the unhealed violence in me, the aggression that can be deeply destructive, I am conscious that it is not only hypocritical to pray for the peace of the world until I have acknowledged as much of my own non-peace as I can recognise but, more important, it is likely to be poor prayer at best and dangerous prayer at worst. For unless I recognise my own violent instincts, there is a danger that they will contaminate my prayer, my deepest longings for the human spirit.

Once we have dealt with that—which perhaps makes it sound simpler and more contained than many of us find it to be—the next hurdle is likely to be an overwhelming sense of helplessness. 'Whatever can I do?' we wail, as we contemplate the deeply ingrained values of false masculinity and aggressiveness at every level of our society. The answer seems blindingly obvious: nothing. If however we believe that God is calling his people forward from the centuries-old domination of the male culture of militarism to a new creation, a new time in which justice, compassion and tenderness—classically, notice, the female virtues—are more significant than brute strength or military fire-power, then to allow ourselves to be disabled by our own sense of inadequacy or powerlessness is to deny the power of God to act in our own history. We need to find within us a prayerful trustingness that he is at work in his world. His grace is sufficient—and it is made perfect in weakness.

It might be good to dwell in prayer on examples of where you have seen that happening, even in microscopic form: a parent whose authority is never buttressed by violence; a husband who is in touch with the feminine side of his own personality and is delivered from false models of maleness; a policeman who refuses to be corrupted by the prevailing culture of authoritarianism and controlled aggression. That is where the values of the kingdom are being lived and struggled for—and every example you can think of needs your prayerful support. For the corrosive acids of our culture are gnawing away at them.

But you will want to go further than that. Without prejudging the interaction which you can only find for yourself between the action and the prayer components of the cycle, there are two areas you might like to include in your prayer that may not come automatically from the action in which you are engaged. The first is prayer for those who are trying to fashion and live non-violent forms of protest and conflict management. From Ghandi to the Witness for Peace to the White Train to Greenham Common, there is a trail of those who have not shirked the tension of conflict, but have refused to solve those conflicts by resorting to violence. In South Africa, the Philippines, Europe and the United States courageous people are joining that trail day by day. They need all the prayer and spiritual empathy we can give them.

Second, we have seen again and again that fear is the beginning of violence. It may be helpful to look for examples of fear being overcome by the slower and more costly process of building relationships that move from suspicion to trust, to care, to love.

Such examples might be found in relationships between different ethnic groups; between different age groups; between people with different views; just occasionally people from different churches. To own and encourage those processes in prayer is a first step to holding in meditative longing the vision offered in the last two readings at the beginning of this chapter.

For that is where prayer for peace is going to come out—with the vision of a glorious Christ who makes all things new; and all things One.

## ACTION

**1.** Start where you have the right to be heard—in your own church. Look again at the liturgy. Where are prayer for peace and for the overthrow of the values of violence properly respected? How much imagination and liturgical creativity is brought to bear? Is there room for improvement? How can that be brought about in a way that genuinely enables the whole people of God to join in the intercessions and the thanksgiving?

**2.** What about the teaching ministry of the church? How aware are the teachers, both ordained and lay? Does the teaching ever get beyond wingeing about violence on television? How can you help it to move further?

**3.** There is no shortage of movements you can join both to keep you in touch with what is going on and to suggest programmes of action. They range from the Campaign for Nuclear Disarmament to the Fellowship of Reconciliation.

**4.** This is a complex field—at least at the level of the politics and strategies of disarmament—and you may well feel that you need to keep up to date. You may also feel that you need alternative sources of information against which to test the often politically loaded materials of the campaigning groups. One of the most respected bodies in the field is the Stockholm International Peace Research Institute, which publishes an authoritative annual Yearbook. Less formidable is the Life and Peace Institute in Uppsala, Sweden. This is a more specifically Christian group which publishes a thoughtful newsletter on many of the key issues. In the UK, peace research is still a neglected field, and one that some ignorant voices from the yob-tendency of the Far Right seek to vilify. The

Illiteracy is a major problem in the Third World, especially among women. Many Third World countries are now working hard to combat this in a bid to solve wider social problems. These women are at an adult literacy course in Kitui, Kenya.

university of Bradford has one of the oldest established University Departments on Peace Studies and is a considerable national resource.

**5.** Many surveys show just how frightened and under-informed the British public is on many of these issues. To encourage a better informed public debate, avoiding the stereotypes and trying to face the facts courageously and honestly, is something that is always worth doing. But it is not easy—for reasons we have already explored. It may well be wise, therefore, to start the process in an environment where mutual acceptance is sufficiently strong to bear the weight of this kind of discussion.

**6.** The real objective is not just to change policies but to change the values that lie behind those policies. Television is undoubtedly a very powerful medium that helps form values, and therefore a television monitoring group can play a useful role. Television awareness training has unfortunately not taken off in the UK in the way that it has in the US: none the less some Church affiliated bodies do offer it. Notice that the object is not only to complain about unnecessary portrayals of violence and objectionable forms of the macho imagery that lie behind it: it is much more to encourage a positive approach to the counter values that will finally replace violence. For example, look for and express appreciation of reporting of non-violent forms of resistance; of creative forms of conflict management; of expressions of dissent from the prevailing ideology; of attempts to present positive images of 'the enemy', whether that be Russia, Iran, Argentina or any other people we are officially encouraged to hate and despise.

**7.** In the same way, one small step in peace making is often becoming acquainted with, and encouraging others to become acquainted with, 'the other'—the person or group, that is, who is usually represented as the foe. This can take a variety of forms—from 'alternative' tourism to simply asking a local representative of the other—perhaps a student—in for a cup of tea and giving them the opportunity to talk about their homeland. What is at stake here is the rejection of 'official' stereotypes, first in our own minds, then throughout as much of the community as we can reach.

**8.** To finish on something more basic in every sense: how good it would be if we could all, once and for all, get away from toys and games that glorify violence. You might think that after two World Wars and umpteen proxy wars, that would be a readily agreed agenda. A visit to any toy shop in December affords a sad commentary on the celebration of the birth of the Prince of Peace ... so if you want something hard edged to start with, why not picket the toy shops in your area, before they buy their stock for Christmas?

## APPRAISAL

This is the part of the cycle where we go back and look at how the other components—reflection on the love of God, analysis, prayer and action are fitting together. The great temptation is to appraise only the effectiveness of what we have been doing, as though the kingdom of heaven were won by our effective actions. It isn't. It is made possible only by our capacity to love, suffer and endure.

An area that might be particularly relevant in the appraisal associated with militarism and violence is the interaction of our reflection on the love of God and our deepening awareness of the issues as they are revealed by the analytical work we are able to do. There are times when it will seem impossible to us that God can go on loving a world so locked into hatred, brutality and murder. Indeed, we will be tempted to despise him for his perseverance:

why on earth doesn't he just give up and leave us to blow ourselves to bits? We are back, with a vengeance, to the love of God as witnessed by St John and St Paul. He is not finally that kind of God. He is rather, incredibly, one who never lets go, who never gives up.

If we can really get hold of that, not only in our minds but in our hearts, at gut level, we will find that we are well on the way to the actions I described in the last section. For much of the time it will feel that we are making no progress at all; that we are simply not heard; that even the institutional Church is so cautious and middle-of-the-road that it can give us no real support.

Without being romantic about it—for it can be hell—I would want to say that that is a good place to be. That is not to glorify failure and ineffectiveness, but rather to recognise that when we have done our best and achieved next to nothing, we are sharing, in however remote a way, something of the pain of the Trinity as they wait for the completion of the work of redemption. If we feel frustrated, they feel frustrated. If we feel let down, they feel let down. If we feel discouraged and lonely ... well, that is something like it must have felt on Golgotha. There is a danger that such a line of thinking can be easily perverted into a sentimental self-indulgence; so watch it. But avoid thinking that you are alone in knowing what it is to hit rock bottom and to be sickened by the self-destructiveness of humanity. You are not. And he who shares it with you still offers as his face to the world the smile of accepting love.

Chapter Five

# TECHNOLOGY

## REFLECTION ON THE LOVE OF GOD

READ EXODUS 35:30–36

Moses said to the sons of Israel, 'See, Yahweh has singled out Bezalel son of Uri, son of Hur, of the tribe of Judah. He has filled him with the spirit of God and endowed him with skill and perception and knowledge for every kind of craft: for the art of designing and working in gold and silver and bronze; for cutting stones to be set, for carving in wood, for every kind of craft. And on him and Oholiab son of Ahisamach, of the tribe of Dan, he has bestowed the gift of teaching. He has filled them with skill to carry out all the crafts of engraver, damask weaver, embroiderer in purple stuffs, of violet shade and red, in crimson stuffs and fine linen, or of the common weaver; they are able to do work of all kinds, and to do it with originality'.

A relatively late account of the building of the Mosaic sanctuary for the ark, this passage is central to the biblical understanding of technical skill.

First, the skill of Bezalel and Oholiab is the gift of God. Yahweh chooses to whom the gift may be given, and it is a gift associated with 'the spirit of God'. No doubt the author has in mind the context of the particular job in hand, the construction of the sanctuary, but our contemporary division between sacred and secular work has no parallel in the Bible. Weaver, engraver, designer, goldsmith, metalsmith ... all the creative skills come from God and his Spirit.

Second, skill is not enough. Along with skill goes 'perception' (35:31; 36:1). Skill is balanced by a wider knowledge, an ability to 'see' reality, to 'perceive' the context in which the skill is set. Perception is allied with appreciation of wholeness (36:1). Technique, then, cannot be divorced from wisdom, a theme to which we shall return in the analytical section.

Third, technique is not to be grasped and clung on to: it is to be shared. Teaching (35:34) is thus the mirror image of technical brilliance.

Fourth, technique is developed by the application of original thinking, of creativity, of courageous innovation (35:35). By comparison with the highly stylised art forms of contemporary cultures, the author stresses that the gift of technical skill brings with it the challenge of originality.

Fifth, the Spirit who gives technical skill also gives abundance (36:5). The author has his own reason for emphasising the generosity of the people in contributing to the project, but we need to honour the fact that both Old and New Testaments point to a God who is not embarrassed by plenty, even excess. Meanness and narrow-spirited asceticism are not the marks of the Spirit.

READ GENESIS 3:17–19

To the man he said, 'Because you listened to the voice of your wife and ate from the tree of which I had forbidden you to eat,

'Accursed be the soil because of you.
With suffering shall you get your food from it
every day of your life.
It shall yield you brambles and thistles,
and you shall eat wild plants.
With sweat on your brow
shall you eat your bread,
until you return to the soil,
as you were taken from it.
For dust you are
and to dust you shall return.'

These familiar verses repay renewed study. In contrast to the blessing of skill, wisdom and abundance in the last reading, the nature of the human lot is here represented as sweat, suffering and dry bread. The contrast could hardly be sharper.

We may want to ponder three implications. First, degrading drudgery is a curse. There is nothing fine or beautiful about it. Its end is to separate men and women from the knowledge of the love of God (3:19). Those who romanticise Victorian values, beware.

Second, the curse is the result of disobedience, that is, of the neglect of the moral demands of Yahweh's reign. Behind this key idea in the religion of Israel lie two central convictions. Moral inadequacy imposes its own penalty, and that penalty is not a spiritualised, other-worldly loss: it is pain and grief and horror in the most basic preoccupations of life.

Third, the curse is on the whole of humanity. For one section to escape it while others remain caught in it is to fly in the face—again—of the 'knowledge of good and evil'. More concretely, the use of technology to escape drudgery—to move from the curse of Genesis to the blessing of Exodus—has to take account of the justice of Yahweh, with its particular compassion for the weak and vulnerable.

READ JEREMIAH 27:4–11

'Give them the following message for their masters, "Yahweh Sabaoth, the God of Israel, says this: You must tell your masters this: I by my great power and outstretched arm made the earth, man and the animals that are on earth. And I can give it to whom I please. For the present, I have handed all these countries over to Nebuchadnezzar king of Babylon, my servant; I have even put the wild animals at his service. (All the nations will be subject to him, to his son and to his grandson, until the time for his own country comes in its turn, when mighty nations and great kings will enslave him.) Any nation or kingdom that will not submit to Nebuchadnezzar king of Babylon, and will not bow its neck to the yoke of the king of Babylon, I shall punish with sword, famine and plague—it is Yahweh who speaks—until I have delivered it into his power. For your own part, do not listen to your prophets, your diviners, dreamers, soothsayers, or sorcerers, who tell you: You will not be subjects of the king of Babylon. They prophesy lies to you, the result of which will be that you will be banished from your soil, that I shall expel you, and you will perish. The nation, however, that bends its neck to the yoke of the king of Babylon and submits to him, I shall leave in peace on its own soil—it is Yahweh who speaks—to farm it and stay in it.'"

Historically, this prophecy comes at the time when Judah was threatened with defeat and exile by Nebuchadnezzar—around 593 BC. For us, however, its interest lies less in its historical context than in the religious consciousness it portrays. Four elements stand out:

☐ First is the conviction that Yahweh is the Lord of history and of the whole natural order. Nothing is beyond him, or hidden from him, or unknown to him. Here is vibrant belief in a God of action, of intervention, of self-disclosure.

☐ Second, he is a God who is not limited by convention or natural expectations. He even chooses Nebuchadnezzar, the heathen, the scourge of God's people, as his servant. He is thus the God of paradox, who saves those who take the course of action that scandalises the conventional, and who punishes those who live by the prevailing wisdom.

☐ Third, in 27:7 we get a glimpse of the notion of the kairos. The right time comes. There is a moment in history ... Babylon's time of crisis is not yet; but it will come.

☐ Fourth, it therefore follows that 'knowing the times', 'discerning the signs' is crucial. Who do you listen to? The conventional experts (v.9): or the word of God (v.11)? And how do you tell one from the other?

As we shall see later in this chapter, those are contemporary questions. Like the just person in Jerusalem in 593, we are surrounded by a babble of voices, offering conflicting (and usually soothing) advice. 'Leave it to the experts. They know.' Yet we sense a dangerous moment; a kairos or crisis full of paradox and perplexity. Perhaps we need more than ever to be assured of a God who acts in history and thereby continues to reveal himself as a God of love.

READ JOHN 12:31–32

'Now sentence is being passed on this world;
now the prince of this world is to be overthrown.
And when I am lifted up from the earth,
I shall draw all men to myself.'

The central Christian affirmation is that Christ's death and resurrection changes human history. Through Christ's life, death and rising again, the curse of Adam is set aside and new possibilities of life are offered to the whole community.

These verses are appropriate here for two reasons. First, we often assume, along with many of our contemporaries, that what will *really* make a difference to the human condition is human ingenuity. Clever doctors offer us longer life; clever technicians more gadgets; clever chemists and physicists more resources ... We too easily forget or ignore 'the prince of this world'.

Second, St John, like St Paul and the early Church, believed that Christ had overcome 'the prince of this world'. The satanic forces of evil had been routed—and it was now the Church's task to live the life of the Spirit to show what that means. We shall find that this tension between the values of Satan and the values of the kingdom lies near the heart of the most important debates about technology. The prince of this world has indeed been overthrown on the cross: but he can play the very devil with our lives by enthroning his values in our technologies.

READ MARK 2:1–12

When he returned to Capernaum some time later, word went round that he was back; and so many people collected that there was no room left, even in front of the door. He was preaching the word to them when some people came bringing him a paralytic carried by four men, but as the crowd made it impossible to get the man to him, they stripped the roof over the place where Jesus was; and when they had made an opening, they lowered the stretcher on which the paralytic lay. Seeing their faith, Jesus said to the paralytic, 'My child, your sins are forgiven.' Now some scribes were sitting there, and they thought to themselves, 'How can this man talk like that? He is blaspheming. Who can forgive sins but God?' Jesus, inwardly aware that this was what they were thinking, said to them, 'Why do you have these thoughts in your hearts? Which of these is easier: to say to the paralytic, "Your sins are forgiven" or to say, "Get up, pick up your stretcher and walk"? But to prove to you that the Son of Man has authority on earth to forgive sins,'—he said to the paralytic—'I order you: get up, pick up your stretcher, and go off home.' And the man got up, picked up his stretcher at once and walked out in front of everyone, so that they were all astounded and praised God saying, 'We have never seen anything like this.'

Although we shall not be considering medical technology in any detail in this chapter, this story is none the less directly relevant to many of the questions we shall have to address. For it reminds us of the false polarities that our science-dominated culture so readily makes between 'body' and 'spirit'. As we saw in the Old Testament readings, the Bible is always aware of the need to hold together not only the whole human personality, but also the whole created order ... and *therefore* to ally technology with wisdom, technique with perception.

The implications of this passage go far beyond medicine. Once we rediscover a vision of the essential unity of creation, many of our technological solutions cease to look like solutions at all. Indeed the very notion that we can 'run the world' by proceeding from one technical fix to another begins to look suspiciously like blasphemy—exactly the sin the scribes, caught in their own one-dimensional world, threw at Jesus.

You might care to spend time on the last two verses. Notice how Jesus pokes fun at his critics by doing what they want him to do—that is, work a 'normal' cure—but does it to illustrate exactly what they want to deny: that health cannot be confined to mechanical function. To his critics' fury, 'everyone' is 'astounded'.

READ 1 CORINTHIANS 11:23–27

For this is what I received from the Lord, and in turn passed on to you: that on the same night that he was betrayed, the Lord Jesus took some bread, and thanked God for it and broke it, and he said, 'This is my body, which is for you; do this as a memorial of me.' In the same way he took the cup after supper, and said, 'This cup is the new covenant in my blood. Whenever you drink it, do this as a memorial of me.' Until the Lord comes, therefore, every time you eat this bread and drink this cup, you are proclaiming his death, and so anyone who eats the bread or drinks the cup of the Lord unworthily will be behaving unworthily towards the body and blood of the Lord.

It may seem surprising to be invited to reflect on the Last Supper as preparation for thinking about technology. What is the connection? There are at least four.

☐ Bread is a symbol of work. It is no accident that at the heart of all Christian worship lies a symbol that captures the ambiguity of our working lives: sweat and nourishment. Bread, however, represents more than sweat: it represents skill in growing, harvesting and baking. We do not offer half-baked bread to be for us the body of Christ. We are thus faced with another ambiguity: hard work and human creativity blended to produce the finest offering.

☐ Wine is a symbol of leisure and pleasure. It is, then, the mirror image of bread. For it is relief from slog, recreation after the pressure of creativity. It is denied to those who have to work too hard, too long for too little; or to those who, whether for internal or external reasons, make work a drug. If our technology robs people of a proper freedom from work, how can we offer the wine of leisure?

☐ In the Lord's Supper we believe that these symbols are embued with the life of Christ. In what sense is the world of work and leisure, the world in which most of us spend most of our time, 'embued with the life of Christ'? That raises wider questions than technology alone: but when we consider the technologies associated with communications, advertising, health, fertility, food production and energy it becomes apparent that we cannot separate 'technology' from 'life'. If it is proper to discern Christ in 'life', it is no less proper to discern him in the technologies that undergird that life.

□ Bread and wine in the Lord's Supper are blessed, broken—and shared. There is enough for everyone, as St Paul insists in his teaching to the Corinthians. If there is not enough to go round, then those who partake are celebrating 'unworthily'. They are denying the worth, the value, the central essence, of what they are doing. If the Lord's Supper is a mirror of the whole of life and not just a cultic ritual, that has profound implications for some of the key questions about the control, accessibility and targets of technology with which we shall be wrestling in the rest of this chapter.

## ANALYSIS

Technical progress has three key features. It is accelerating: compare the 'technological distance' covered in the first twenty years of this century and the last twenty. It is becoming more complex: look at the lists of specialisms in any decent-sized hospital. And it is unpredictable. For example, although the National Resources Committee of the United States Department of the Interior produced a report in 1937 which is still remarkable for its scope and foresight, even it failed adequately to identify five fundamental technologies that would appear within the next ten years: atomic energy, computers, radar, antibiotics and the jet engine. Within the lifetime of any reader of this book it is absolutely certain that technologies will appear that none of us can now visualise.

Sometimes we think of technology as something 'out there', as though, that is, technology has an independent existence like the moon or the wind or the monarchy. The reality, of course, is that technology plays a major—some people would say *the* major—role in shaping not only institutions and forms of economic and political organisation, but also the language, the structure of social relationships, the distribution of income and wealth and power, even the way we think.

The Industrial Revolution, for instance, did not just change the means of production. It changed the way in which people lived, related to each other and thought about themselves, their world and its future. The telephone, radio and television have not only changed the technology of communication; they have changed the pattern of family life, the structure of friendships and support systems, sources of knowledge, dialect, and the ways in which we think about ourselves, the world and the future. At the risk of beating the point to death, the explosion of atomic bombs in Nagasaki and Hiroshima changed not only military technology, but the whole structure of international relations, and the nature of diplomacy. As some percipient observers commented at the time, it made inevitable the pre-emption of huge resources on a global scale by the arms race.

This chapter cannot, therefore, be about technology alone. Although we shall look at some of the problems posed by hard and soft technologies, we shall find that the kairos questions about technology turn out to be questions not just about technology, but about the kind of society in which we want to live; the ways in which we want to relate to each other; the kinds of community in which we think human fulfilment is most likely to be achieved; the values and ultimates that give to life meaning, structure, hope and creative possibility. About, in a word, the nature of wisdom.

But that is to anticipate ... It is time to look more closely at the range of opinion that has formed round two key questions that must strike us as soon as we begin to reflect upon the role technology plays in our history and our future. Will it work? Will it work for good?

## 1. THE NATURE OF THE DEBATE

Both of those questions need unpacking a little. The first is essentially about the long-run feasibility of technological progress. Are there limits to the nature of problems that technology can solve? Are we seeing at the moment a particularly fruitful period of technological creativity which will be followed by a desert? The great American scholar, Joseph Schumpeter, long ago developed what he called the Bucket Theory of Technical Change. According to Schumpeter, fundamental and applied sciences beaver away accumulating small advances, filling up the bucket of knowledge. When the bucket is full it is automatically emptied in a spate of technical invention. Schumpeter illustrated this with respect to the internal combustion engine and the electric motor, both of which allowed rapid progress as these particular inventions were applied across a broad spectrum of activity. In our own day, the discovery of DNA and the development of techniques to

When Robert Oppenheimer, developer of the first atom bomb, saw the first test bomb explode, words from the Bhagavad-Gita, sacred to Hindus, came to his mind: 'I am become Death, the shatterer of worlds'. The skill of humanity has brought us to this point.

manipulate DNA through genetic engineering techniques are likely to have the same effect.

Now if the bucket theory operates over a ten to twenty year period, is it not conceivable that a mega bucket is operating in the nineteenth and twentieth centuries, with the result that humankind may have to wait a very long time before the mega bucket refills, perhaps in the twenty-first and twenty-second centuries?

Another set of anxieties about the feasibility of technology surround what has come to be known as the 'limits to growth'. This was the title of a famous study by the Meadows, which, in the early seventies, was given great prominence by the prestigious Club of Rome. On the basis of modelling techniques that are now seen to be crude and simplistic, the Meadows argued that the world would run into absolute limits in terms of resources, heat transfer and population pressure within the next century. For example, suppose there are no safe energy technologies that can exploit renewable sources of energy. Then we are heading up a blind alley and all technology does, perhaps, is lead us faster to the end of that alley.

A final set of questions about the feasibility of technology have to do with its sustainability and safety. It has become a cliché to see the development of nuclear power as a Faustian bargain. Perhaps we have bought salvation from the constraints of non-renewable energy sources, but at a price that means we live under the shadow of Chernobyl. Indeed, much of the ecological debate which we have already reviewed in some detail betrays the same kind of anxiety. Will the development of the supersonic aircraft industry destroy the ozone layer? Will the consumption of more and more energy melt the polar ice cap? Will the development of irrigation technologies be self-defeating because they will destroy the irrigated soils? All these are examples of technological pessimism because they assume that, in the end, technology leads us up blind alleys from which there is no escape, technological or otherwise.

These anxieties are given greater power when they are put in the context of the three leading characteristics of modern technology with which we started this chapter—speed, complexity and unpredictability. Those who raise questions about the long-term feasibility of technological development do so from a deep unease about the way in which those three features interact on each other. Is the exponential rate of increase of technological advance here to stay? Or does the very complexification of technology guarantee a slow down precisely at the point in which the world is exposed to enormous technological risks through, for example, overdependence upon a nuclear power technology that proves to be inherently unsafe?

Although these are important questions on which there is a wide variety of informed opinion, as well as much under-informed near hysteria, it is the second question—'Will technology work for good?'—that has caught the attention of philosophers in general and Christians in particular. We need to unpack it rather carefully because it turns out to have many angles.

We could rephrase the question like this: who benefits from technology? Is there any guarantee that technology will deliver benefits to those in the greatest need? Or is it more likely that the benefits of technology will satisfy the whims of the already privileged while leaving untouched the basic needs of the under-privileged? Will technology, in short, help to create a world that is more recognisably a world of justice, harmony and generosity: or is there something inherent in the very nature of modern technology that will make those virtues more unattainable?

This quickly shades into a cluster of questions about the control of technology. Who determines research priorities? In medicine, for example, where does the bulk of research money go—into problems that are scientifically interesting (like organ transplants), or into problems that inflict pain and anguish to large numbers of people—like the degenerative diseases or, in a global context, diarrhoea, malaria and preventable communicable diseases? Again, we are back to speed, complexity and unpredictability. For what looks like an esoteric problem in pure science today can quickly but unpredictably become a technology of wide interest and life enhancing quality tomorrow. When it was first developed, for example, fibre optics looked like a technology in search of a use. By the end of the century, it will be fundamental to nearly all telecommunication systems and much diagnostic surgery.

Around these two sets of questions—'Will it work?' and 'Is it benign?'—we can arrange at least four schools of thought.

First of all, there are those, perhaps most notoriously represented by Buckminster Fuller and the Hudson Institute, who would answer both sets of questions with a determined affirmative. They would argue that technology is the epitome of human creativity, and that there is no reason to assume that the capacity of the human intellect to solve technical problems is limited. That is not, of course, to say that every technology is infinitely open to further refinement, or that every technology is worth developing: it is to say that, given time and resources, technical solutions can be found to technical problems with sufficient predictability and confidence to make anxieties about scarcity of resources or some kind of technological Armageddon irrational and therefore unacceptable.

In the same way, Fuller and his disciples argue that technology has already brought a higher standard of living, a higher physical quality of life, and greater possibility for leisure, creativity, artistic expression and human interchange at least in the industrialised countries than would have been conceivable even a hundred years ago. They argue that as the technologies that are already available are applied to the problems of the less developed countries, so they too will be able to enjoy the fruits of technological development. They point to the fact that India has been transformed from a food deficit to a food surplus country by a series of technological innovations which, seen in the context of the whole gamut of technological development over the last thirty years, appear tiny and scientifically unexciting. They point to the eradication of smallpox and the control of malaria, both achieved through very low levels of technological development. They see the political and institutional underdevelopment of the Third World as constituting the major constraint on its development: if those constraints were solved, technology could deliver to the whole of mankind a level of living which would allow the further development of human capacities of all sorts.

Surprising bedfellows of the right wing Hudson Institute are many commentators from the Soviet Union. Y. D. Modrzhinskaya and C. A. Stephanyan, in their book *The Future of Society* (Moscow, 1973) set out at length why they reject western anxieties about the application of technology in the future. Predictably, they argue that the downfall of the capitalist system is needed in order to liberate the potential power of technology to transform society under the revolutionary movement of communism. Although they quote Lenin's caution about seeing history as an uninterrupted line of progress—'it is undialectical, unscientific and theoretically wrong to regard the course of world history as smooth and always in a forward direction without occasional gigantic leaps back'—they are confident that mankind's ingenuity can ensure steady progress.

> Over the last twenty to thirty years, the pace of scientific and technological development has acquired quite exceptional, hitherto unprecedented, proportions, and it is difficult to imagine with what tremendous speed man's prospects for mastering the forces of nature will develop in the future.

It is thus no surprise to find them expressing absolute disagreement with limits to growth styles of thought:

> Soviet scientists ... categorically reject all theories of future energy shortage and raw material shortage.

Likewise, in agricultural production they expect man to be equally successful, eventually 'turning the desert into flowering orchards'. Although they recognise that scientists have to accept the possible deleterious effects of environmental intervention, they none the less set out future tasks of daunting scale, including the damming of the Bering Straits in order to conquer the Arctic permafrost.

If these extreme right and extreme left commentators can give such unqualified affirmative answers to the two fundamental questions we are posing, it is perhaps a surprise to find other voices that give a no less unqualified negative reply to both questions.

I have already referred to the Meadows study, *Limits to Growth*. Both they and J. W. Forrester produced models in the late sixties and early seventies which, on the basis of the continuation of present trends—particularly in terms of population growth—forecast a collapse of global economic, ecological and political systems in the next century.

The details of the argument need not detain us here: for our purposes, what is important is to see that both of these authors argue that there is no *technological* solution to social and political systems which make population growth unstoppable. Like Malthus, the 'dismal scientist' who argued that population growth always tends to outgrow food supply, Forrester and Meadows argue that technology is powerless to overcome the strain on the earth's resources posed by present levels of population growth. Malthus forecast the so-called 'Malthusian check', a euphemism for massive famine that will bring the level of population back within the carrying capacity of the land (a forecast that looked horribly true from the perspective of Ireland decimated by the potato famine of the 1840s). Meadows and Forrester foresee the collapse of existing economic and political systems which will have exactly the same effect, that is, reduce global population to a sustainable level. And that, they argue, technology is powerless to prevent. Here we are in a world as far removed from the optimism of the Hudson Institute and Modrzhinskaya as it is possible to imagine.

For modern Malthusians, questions about the distribution of the benefits of technology hardly arise. But to some other authors who share their alarm at the inability of technology to solve resources constraints, the distribution of the benefits of technology is the key question. Thus both Schumacher and the Ehrlichs see an overdeveloped, uncontrolled technology as raising the problems of resource scarcity to a higher power. The Erlichs recommend *de*-development in rich countries with the rapid adoption of low level technologies that conserve resources. Schumacher diagnoses the essential problem as the choice of scale of technology, recommending the simplification and humanisation of technology precisely in order to ensure that it serves the essential needs of humankind rather than the less essential needs of political and technological elites.

With the possible exception of Schumacher, the authors I have quoted so far have been primarily concerned with the role of technology in the future. Perhaps technology's most trenchant critics—particularly with respect to the second of our questions, 'Is technology benign?'—are less concerned with the future than with the present. What drives these critics is the fear that questions about the benign or malign nature of technology are meaningless. For if we ask whether technology is benign we assume that there is some kind of moral control on technology. The radical critics of technology fear that such moral controls do not and—such is the nature of technology—*cannot* exist. Technology is thus out of moral control, responding to its own inner laws, determining its own future. Thus Jacques Ellul, 'The technical phenomenon has assumed an independent character quite apart from economic considerations ... it develops according to its own intrinsic laws ... following its own intrinsic causal processes independent of external forces or human aims.'

Others would argue that while it may be true that both pure and applied sciences have their own inner dynamic, it is precisely the 'economic considerations' dismissed by Ellul that ensure not only the dynamism of technology but also its mismatch with human needs. The increasing concentration of the control of research and development resources into the hands of, first, the military, and, second, the largest multinational corporations, tends to ensure that benefits of technology serve those controlling interests: namely the military, and the oligarchs who run the larger multinational corporations. The former are professionally interested in destruction; the latter are professionally interested in profits. Neither is nor can be interested in controlling technology to deliver benefits to those whose needs are greatest and whose ability to pay is the most slender.

Nor can they be interested in the consequences of the technological choices that they make which lie outside their area of responsibility. The military cannot be interested in the long-term effects of nuclear weapon tests, for example, in the Pacific. The industrial technocrats cannot be interested in acid rain in Europe, or iatrogenic diseases in the Third World. For such effects are external to their area of responsibility. And they are usually powerful enough to ensure that attempts to internalise those effects—for example, by 'making the polluter pay'—are rendered useless.

Whether the uncontrollability of technology comes, as someone like Ellul would maintain, from its own inner dynamic, or as Schumacher and Roszak would argue, from the economic imperatives within which technology is set, the fundamental issue remains the same: technology is perceived as possessed by a power that defies democratic control.

Between the extreme pessimism of people like Ellul and Roszak and the naive optimism of Fuller and Modrzhinskaya lie two views that I want to touch on briefly. The first is best expressed by Bertrand de Juvenal, one of the first people to bring a wide range of intellectual disciplines to bear on the study of the future. Dismissing Ellul's fears as 'impotent and paradoxical technophobia', Juvenal has this to say:

> Membership of a technologically advanced and advancing society is unquestionably a privilege. It is true of all privileges that they can be put to good or bad use. In this case it is quite clear that the privilege is collective by nature, that the benefits and the evils depend a great deal more upon aggregate behaviour than upon individual decisions.

For Juvenal, then, the issue is not the inner essence of technology. Nor is it a kind of economic determinism that sees technology as inevitably controlled by the profit maximising drive of ever larger, ever less controllable corporations. The fundamental issue for Juvenal is the nature of 'aggregate behaviour'. How do societies respond to the challenge and opportunities bestowed by the technological possibilities that are becoming available to them? He is critical of Ellul because he fears—what Ellul denies—that such pessimism leads to despair and therefore a refusal to take responsibility. And he would be dismissive of the ultra optimists because they are so optimistic that they do not see the ambiguity of technology. They therefore reject a moral imperative to take collective responsibility for its development and application.

Dennis Goulet comes to the same conclusion via a very different route. Goulet has spent much of his life as a participant observer among 'poor' and 'primitive' peoples from the Navajos in the United States to the Romany peoples in Europe. He sees a radical discontinuity between, on the one hand, the way in which these so-called primitive societies are structured, with the primacy of human values that make possible genuine community and the creation and sustenance of deep wisdom that gives meaning to life, death, joy and suffering, and, on the other hand, the alienation, anomie, violence and meaninglessness of life in the societies of industrialised countries dominated by technology and the values derived from it.

For Goulet, then, the central issue is not whether technology will work or even whether it can be made benign. The central question '... is not technology *itself*, but the successful *management* of it which requires wisdom and clarity as to the kind of society desired, and the ways in which technology can help construct it.'

Goulet sees technology as both a bearer and a destroyer of values. He fears that the values that it bears are inconsistent with the values that finally sustain human happiness and fulfilment, just as surely as the values that it destroys—community, mutuality, generosity, patience, gentleness—conduce to it.

For Goulet, then, every technological question is ultimately a question of values: of what is ultimately important; of what individuals and societies live for, die for, and hope to be redeemed from. But Goulet recognises that the choice of values to be embodied in technology and in society at large is not easy or conflict free. He argues, however, that the conflict that surrounds those value choices—and therefore that surrounds the choice of technology—can prove beneficial, because they make individuals and societies clarify and enunciate the values at stake.

> The key lies in the criteria chosen to decide which values will be destroyed, and which will be preserved. Technology is indeed a two-edged sword, at once beneficent and destructive. But so is ... all of human history.

For Goulet, then, taking responsibility for the privilege of technology, as Bertrand Juvenal would put it, involves facing the ambiguity not only of technology but of the values that are to be incorporated both in the technology and in society at large. Choice of technology, according to Goulet, is not exclusively or even primarily a technical assessment to be made within the universe of discourse of technologists alone. The choice of what technology to use, of what technology to develop, of what resources to put in to a search for a particular technical solution—all these are intensely human choices that have to arise out of the clash of explicit values.

Nuclear leaks. Nuclear waste-disposal. Nuclear catastrophes. What constitutes an acceptable standard of safety in the nuclear industry?

It is a short step—and a step that Goulet himself hints at but does not take explicitly—from seeing questions of technology as essentially questions of value, to seeing them as essentially questions of politics. That is to say, the decision about whose values triumph is not a decision that is made purely in terms of the moral

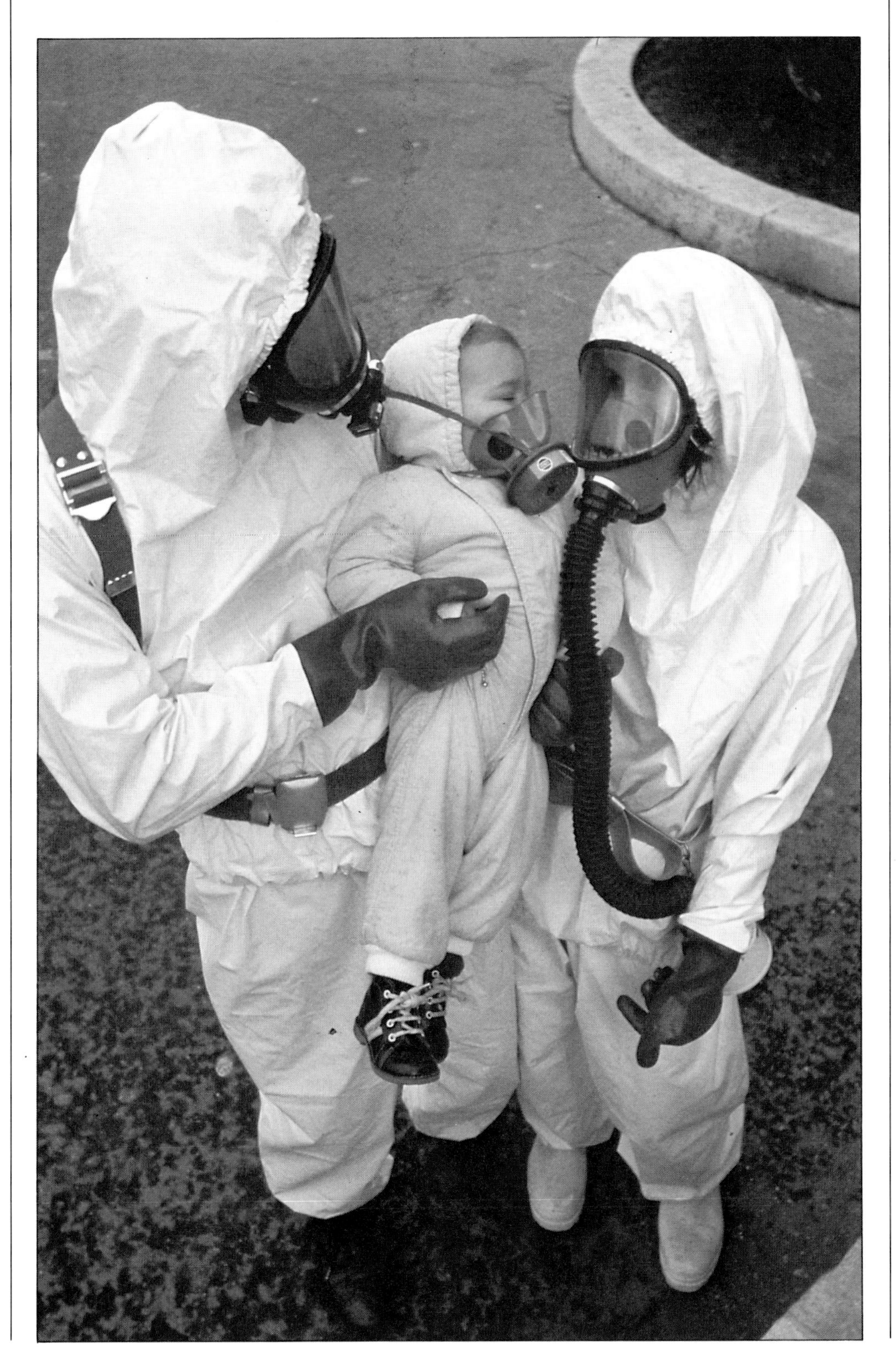

superiority of one set of values over another. Schumacher's vision of technology is not automatically implemented over Modrzhinskaya's just because it is more human and more Christian. On the contrary, Modrzhinskaya's vision is more likely to be implemented because she speaks from the standpoint of the Soviet government, while Schumacher speaks from a position of political isolation. By emphasising the role of values in determining the shape and impact of technology, Goulet leads us inexorably to questions of power. This is a theme to which we will have to return, but before we do it will be helpful to anchor the discussion of this section in some of the more concrete choices that our society has to face.

## 2. TECHNOLOGY, CHOICE AND VALUE: HARD AND SOFT EXAMPLES

### Nuclear power

I make no excuse for starting this section with so obvious an example. For nuclear power raises all the key questions more sharply than perhaps any other technology at the same level of development. Let's start by slightly reinterpreting the two questions that guided us through the last section. 'Will it work?' implies a prior question: 'Is it necessary?'

That question itself has to be unpacked still further. Under what conditions is nuclear power necessary? Necessary for whom? To enable them to do what? We can see immediately how what looked like hard-edged technical questions shade off into questions of value and power. For the critics of nuclear power are quick to point out that nuclear power is not necessary, either in the UK or in the USA, under certain conditions: the development of alternative sources of power, particularly renewable sources such as wind, tidal power, solar power; vastly more efficient use and conservation of energy; greater use of public transport; and the use of energy technologies that are matched in scale and geographical distribution to end-use needs. Thus in an influential study for Friends of the Earth, Amory B. Lovins showed that if these (and a number of other) conditions were met, energy use in the United States in the year 2025 could be reduced to one third of its present trend level, and that not only would there be no need for nuclear power at that low level, but that there would be no need for the use of any non-renewable sources of power at all.

Many would claim that Lovins is over-optimistic: for the purposes of our argument, his very carefully worked calculations show that there is no unique or unambiguous answer to questions

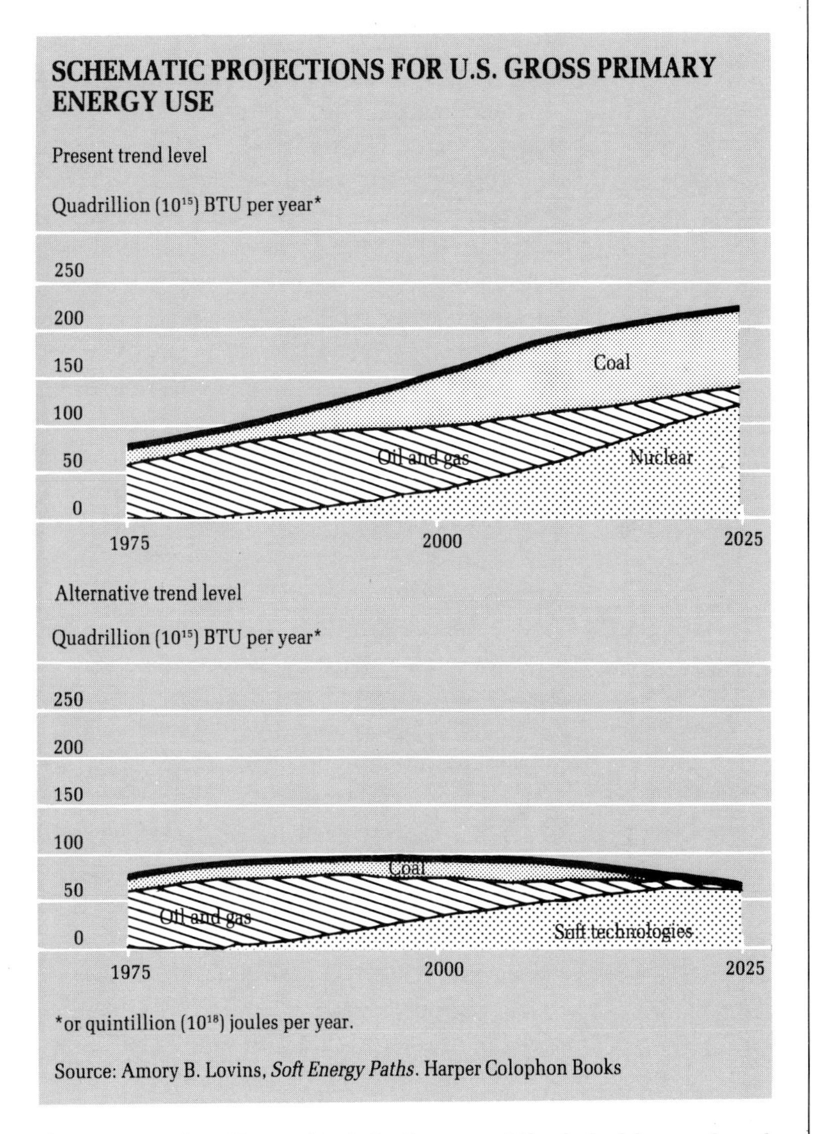


about necessity. Necessity is in the eye of the beholder, and each beholder has to determine for himself or herself what combination of inconvenience, expense, unreliability, risk, environmental hazard and social acceptability is tolerable.

It might seem that the second part of this first question, 'Will it work?'—that is, 'Will it work technically?'—is much more firm-edged. Surely at last we are in to the hard knowable world of the technologist and the scientist. Alas, no. Of course there is a trivial sense in which we know that a number of nuclear power technologies work in the sense that they deliver power. What we don't know are the limits of risk within which they work. Chernobyl and Three Mile Island as well as a vastly larger number of less dramatic incidents make it clear that there are limits within which nuclear power stations 'work'. Those limits change as technologies and operating procedures change: the expectation is that they change for the better. However, even if we knew that there is, let us say, a one-in-a-thousand chance of the meltdown of a nuclear power station in Europe or North America within the next twenty-five years (and most commentators put the chances as much, much higher than that), we still do not know what level of likelihood is acceptable to the public.

There is, of course, a much more pressing sense in which nuclear power can be said not to 'work'. As long as the technology produces radioactive waste which cannot be adequately disposed of, there is a sense in which its 'working' is inadequate or provisional. Very quickly we are back with questions of values and power. It can be put crudely like this: on which section of the community—or of the environment—can the rest of us dump spent nuclear fuel? Are the values of an uncontaminated earth absolute, so that we will tolerate no nuclear dumping anywhere under any conditions? Or are they relative so that the question becomes a technical and economic one about burying radioactive waste deep enough and in sufficiently secure containers as to present a negligible environmental risk? And if the latter, who is actually going to be neighbour to this nuclear waste? And who will decide? And how? The tragicomedy of the British Nuclear Industry's Recycling Executive being forcibly evicted from test drill sites by unlikely alliances of right wing landowners, left wing environmental lobbyists, frightened mothers and outraged grannies shows that the question, 'Will it work?' cannot escape ultimate issues of value and power.

It is, of course, no surprise to find that those issues come even more to the fore when we ask about the distribution of the benefits of nuclear power. Who really gains from the British nuclear power programme? It is hard to argue that nuclear power stations deliver power more cheaply than alternative sources, since the calculation depends critically upon the rate of interest at which the capital is borrowed, and even over quite short periods that can fluctuate by as much as 50 per cent. Certainly there is no absolute economic case for nuclear power, though it is entirely possible to sketch scenarios under which nuclear power can be shown to be economically preferable. But why plump for those scenarios rather than others which can show the reverse?

The industrial arguments—that a successful British nuclear power industry will open up opportunities for the export of the technology—need to be treated with even more caution. Nuclear technology is not British: it is American. And even if it were true

How about it? Workers in declining industries feel isolated and abandoned by the rest of the community.

that a British nuclear power programme will enable British contractors to construct power stations overseas, is it acceptable that the decision to install this technology should be made in order to increase the competitive strength of a number of British companies in this area?

Finally, we come to the 'plurality' argument: that it is in Britain's interest to have a number of sources of power—coal, oil, hydro and nuclear. This boils down to the argument that a source of bargaining strength of the NUM (and presumably the UDM) lies in their ability to close down coal fired power stations, and therefore the development of a nuclear power industry is one way of reducing the power of those unions. Again, notice the value/power dimensions of this argument. At its crudest, it implies that the choice of a technology can legitimately be manipulated to redistribute social and industrial power. Or, to put it another way, it is judged that the environmental and health hazards associated with nuclear power are less than the benefits that society as a whole (or, more likely, the key groups in society that make the choice of the technology) derive from a redistribution of social and political power.

Like surgery, technology becomes ever more sophisticated. But whose job is it to ask what it is all for?

I have put so much emphasis on nuclear power, in the process going over ground that will be familiar to many readers, because it illustrates the kairos nature of the challenge that technology poses us. What sort of society are we trying to create, and what do we reveal about ourselves, both as individuals and as communities, as we make those choices? Those are questions that I shall return to in the second example.

## Biotechnology

We saw in the first section that energy and food have long been identified as the two major constraints on the world's future. In the last section we looked at some of the technical, philosophical and political issues that surround energy supply. It is time now to look at those same issues with respect to food. Biotechnology can, of course, be applied to other areas than food, but I shall concentrate on crop and livestock biotechnologies because they enable us to raise parallel questions to those that we have been examining in the context of nuclear power, but to come at them from a rather wider perspective.

It might be thought that by excluding industrial and, above all, pharmaceutical applications of biotechnologies we are in danger of playing Hamlet without the Prince of Denmark. However, while the lion's share of research and development expenditure in biotechnology is currently devoted to pharmaceuticals, the impact of biotechnology on agriculture over the next twenty years will be impressive. Predictions of global sales of biotechnology-based agricultural products need to be treated with a good deal of caution. But an estimate of global sales of $100 billion per annum by the end of the century are taken seriously within the industry.

With a prospective market of that size it may seem perverse to start by asking the same question as we asked of nuclear power: 'Is this technology really necessary?' Just as a case can be made for saying that we can 'do without' nuclear power by adapting and adopting soft technologies, so a case can be made for arguing that we can do without the biotechnologies associated with food supplies. Only the most extreme pessimists would argue that the world cannot now and will not in the foreseeable future be able to feed itself. At a global level, the real problems of agriculture have much more to do with the distribution of available food than with absolute shortages of supply. That is to say, people go without food not because food is scarce but because their incomes are too low to buy the available food. Only if the new technologies brought the price of food down, or shifted the location of food supply nearer to those who need it, or created agricultural jobs and therefore

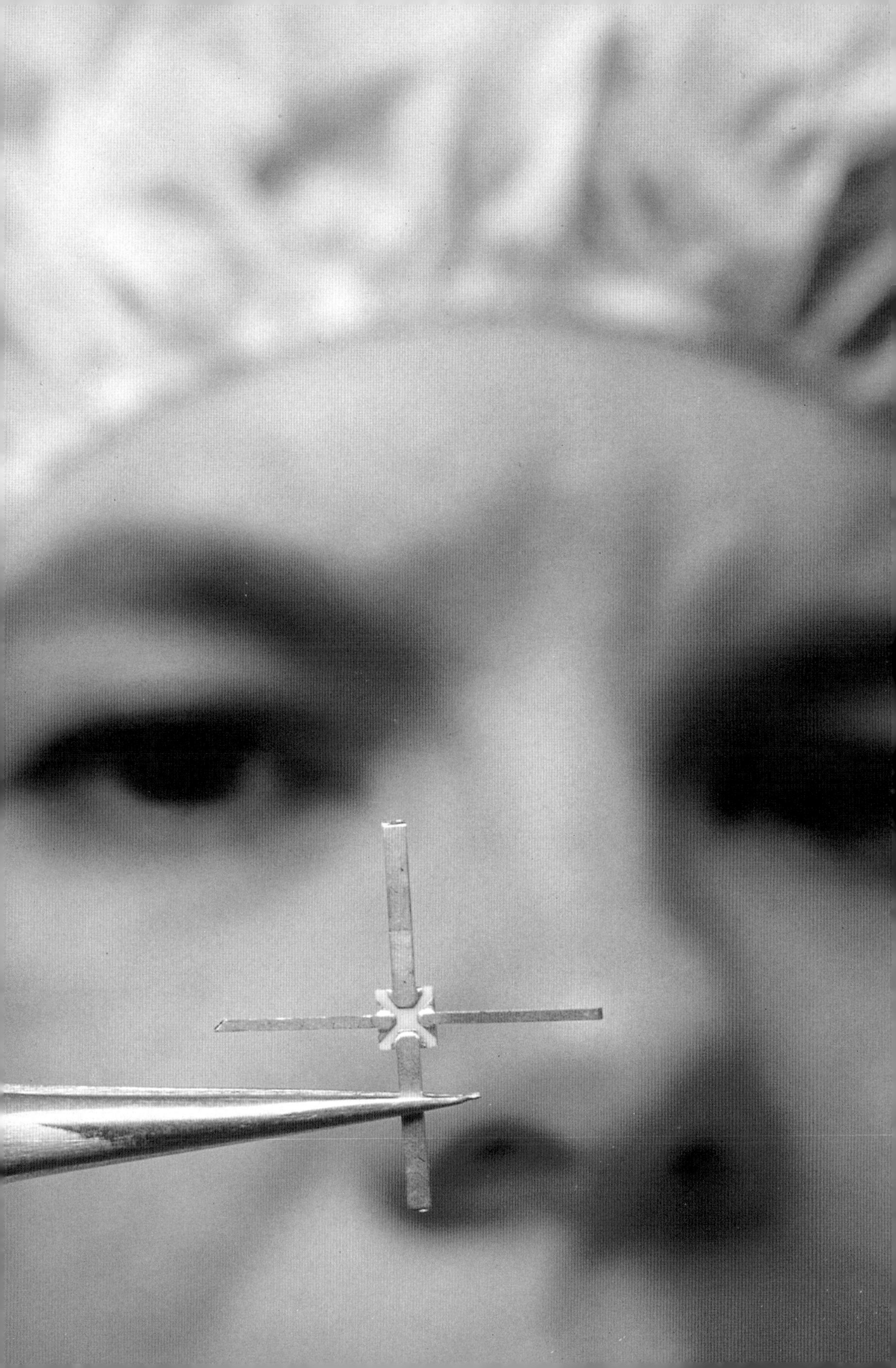

In the 1950s, it was promised that nuclear energy would produce electricity 'too cheap to meter'. In 1986 the dream turned nightmare when the nuclear plant at Chernobyl exploded. Is nuclear power a promise or a threat? Or both?

incomes amongst those currently short of food, could there be a case for saying that these technologies are strictly necessary.

There are some signs that the new technologies will have some of these effects. For example, 60 million hectares of land in South East Asia are affected by high salinity often as a result of intensive irrigation. Furthermore, this huge area is increasing rapidly. If genetic engineering is able to produce varieties of rice with greater saline tolerance—and there is already reason to believe that it will do so—then land that is currently either out of production altogether or producing very poor yields can be made fully productive. In much the same way, much of Brazil's land is affected by severe aluminium toxicity problems which make wheat growing, at best, a marginal possibility. In a country in which hunger for land is, as we have already seen, creating one of the greatest environmental threats in the world, and in which struggles over land are a direct cause of chronic rural violence, the release of seed varieties that can bring in to production marginal land has implications that transcend questions of food supply.

More generally, genetic engineering may be able to do for dry land crops what the green revolution did for irrigated crops. Under optimum conditions—and no one should be in any doubt about the severity of that qualification—high yielding dry land grain varieties could raise the real incomes of very poor people. The question then becomes, 'Is it likely that the varieties that may be produced in the laboratory will in fact be adopted by very poor people?' The history of the green revolution should encourage us to ask that question with our eyes wide open.

For the fact is that most of the genetic engineering that is currently being undertaken, both in terms of saline and toxic resistance and in terms of dry land crops, is being undertaken by the private sector. In contrast to the green revolution, the biotechnological revolution is primarily happening in the research laboratories of corporations who seek to sell the product of the research they are undertaking. For example, the work on aluminium toxicity resistant strains of wheat is confined to seed companies that will seek to sell the seed when it has been proved. It is likely that the seed will be unstable, that is to say, the farmer will not be able to use his own grain as seed in the succeeding year but will be obliged to buy seed afresh. There is plenty of evidence from the green revolution that this acts as a considerable disincentive, especially amongst the poorest farmers, to adoption of the seed in the first place. And that gives substance to the fear that the land will indeed be made productive, but it will be made productive under the ownership and operation of richer farmers, leaving the food deficit families untouched. In that case, the original justification of the technology—namely, that it would increase the supply of food to those who cannot currently afford it—is negated.

Another example makes the same point. In a remarkable scientific achievement, researchers in the US agribusiness firm Calgene isolated, cloned and inserted a gene into cotton plants which conveyed resistance to the widely used herbicide, Roundup. Calgene expects to have Roundup resistant cotton plants in US farmers' fields by 1989, and throughout the world by the mid-nineties. The effect on the sales of Roundup are expected to be dramatic. For the goal of the scientific effort is not to engineer plants requiring less use of herbicide, but rather to create plants that will tolerate increased herbicide use—and thereby save labour on weeding. The effect then is not only to increase the environmental hazards associated with all herbicide use, but more importantly in many developing countries, to reduce the demand for labour and thereby depress agricultural wages and earnings. So far from increasing the availability of food to food deficit families, this technology is likely to reduce it.

Notice, again, the value/power interplay. The values implicit in the development of this technology are that profits for the originators of the technology are more important than hazard to the environment and the displacement of labour. And if it is objected that countries for which the technology is poorly suited can prohibit its import, the track record of technology monitoring is even worse in agricultural chemicals than it is in pharmaceuticals. In a word, poor countries find it extremely hard to keep out unsuitable technologies.

There is, however, a more sinister point behind the privatisation of biotechnology. Increasingly, plant varieties are protected through legal means such as plant variety protection laws or patents. Seeds become 'intellectual property' and, as such, cannot simply be made available to those who need them. And if research organisations in developing countries try to set up their own research laboratories, they soon discover that even the techniques and tools of genetic engineering—including the genes themselves—are patented. This does not mean that they are not available, but that they are available only at a price, and only on the terms dictated by the research companies concerned. As those research companies are linked with the suppliers of agricultural inputs—seeds, fertilisers, chemicals—the payoff almost inevitably means an increased dependence on imported inputs. For the Third World farmer there is indeed no such thing as a free lunch.

It is important, however, to get the nuance right. We are not saying that genetic engineering has no role to play, nor that even privatised genetic engineering has no relevance, or only negative relevance, for the developing world. That is too crude. Rather, we are saying that the values enshrined in these new technologies are of questionable relevance and appropriateness for developing countries. Further, the power that the new technologies give to the firms which originate them cuts across both the political aspirations of the developing countries (to decrease dependence on the West), and the larger values of generosity, kindness and compassion that most of us want to see enshrined in all our relations with people who know what it is to go hungry.

So far I have couched these arguments largely in terms of the relationship between First World biotechnology and Third World agricultural needs. I have done so because that sharpens a more general point; namely, the mismatch or the potential mismatch between biotechnology and social need. That mismatch is not confined to the developing world. It is surely not insignificant that in the two university 'biocentres'—biological research establishments specialising in biotechnology—at British universities in 1985, the major projects were of direct interest to the brewing industry. At Leicester, three research groups were looking at replication and protein secretion in yeasts, and the regulation of gene expression in cucumber seedlings. The interest to brewers of the biochemistry of yeast is obvious, of cucumber seedlings less so. But, in fact, the work on cucumber seedlings is directly related to a piece of genetic engineering that might do away with the need for malting barley, or at least shorten the malting process. At Swansea, the Biotechnology Centre (Wales) was busily developing computer programmes for the automated running of large scale fermenters of the type used by breweries, and had a small scale working model of a brewery fermenter for teaching.

At a time when leaders of the medical profession are pointing to the frightening rise in alcoholism and particularly youth alcoholism, one may legitimately wonder whether technologies designed to improve the efficiency of brewing, and therefore increase the availability of alcohol, reflects social values that have much to do with the real needs of British people. Both biocentres are dependent upon external, that is non-governmental, funding. Their research expertise is therefore market-led—and the market leads to where profits are thought to lie. We are back with values and power.

### Manufacturing technologies

The 'future of work' literature has brought to the public's attention many of the ambiguities of improvements in productive technology in general, and particularly the application of robotics and computer-aided design and manufacture (CADCAM). The dislocation caused by automation and the regressive distribution of its costs (which tend to fall on the elderly, female and immobile) and its benefits (which tend to be annexed by male, young, relatively well-off) are well known, and painfully well illustrated in many parts of Britain's industrial heartland. I want to explore the subject from a somewhat different angle, and thereby raise a set of issues that have not emerged in the two cases I have already examined.

Put briefly, I want to examine the argument that rapid progress in industrial technology (which, of course, is much wider in scope and nature than automation) are inevitable, 'because the others do it'.

This raises the same issue at two distinct levels. Firm A may have to change its productive technology with all that that implies for employment and the local community, because if it doesn't it will be forced out of business by Firm B, which has already adopted the new technology and can now offer a superior product or a lower price. Who wants a washing machine assembled by hand, when one can have a similar machine assembled by robots at 20 per cent discount?

The second level of the same question appears when 'the others' are the Japanese, or the South Koreans, or the West Germans or the Americans. If they adopt a new technology with clear benefits to the consumer, can British producers refuse to do so?

I raise these questions to suggest that the degrees of freedom in choice of technology are not as large as is often assumed. Particularly amongst the most vigorous critics of technological progress, it is often assumed that we are free to adopt or decline to adopt technology without penalty. Very seldom is that the case. Sooner or later—and often, true, it is later rather than sooner—a penalty for technological backwardness has to be paid. It is paid by the firm that goes bust because it can no longer compete. It is paid by the country that loses export markets or is swamped by imports, and has constantly to devalue its currency and thereby erode the living standard of its people.

To put the same thing in a slightly different language and context, it is of the nature of competitive capitalism that pressures are built into the system that encourage the adoption of 'best practice' technology by firms that trade within the same market place. If that market place is the world, then pressures exist for each firm to follow the world technological leader.

In the long run there are only two ways out. Either one can withdraw from the same market place as the technological leader, for example, by putting up tariff barriers or simply denying one's market to the cheap goods from the most efficient producer. Or, one can devalue the currency in order to reduce one's international prices, and so hang on to market share. But that is equivalent to imposing a tax on one's own citizens in order to subsidise the technology leader in one's own country. In other words, to opt out of best practice technology imposes a cost, and either that cost is borne by a firm that opts out or it can be shared amongst society as a whole. Politics will determine who pays the price.

And that is the point. In the end, the distribution of the costs and benefits of technology choice is determined by political processes. But at this point we need to be careful. It is tempting to leave the argument there. To say, in other words, that choices of technology are made by individuals and corporations for their own purposes, perhaps responding to the inner dynamic of technology itself, and certainly responding to competitive pressures, and that once those decisions are made the distribution of the costs and benefits is worked out through the clash of interests in the political arena. Unfortunately the picture isn't quite as simple as that. For the same clash of interests, the same political processes, play a major role in determining the way in which technology is adopted and adapted. We have already seen a little of that at work in the case of nuclear power: that is an entirely political decision in which certainly economic and technical considerations are weighed, but then set in a much wider context. Even such technologies as diagnostic and surgical techniques are the outcome of political decisions; for example, decisions on how much money to put into medical research; how much money to make available to high tech medical teams; how to structure the whole delivery of health care as between curative, preventative and promotive.

Even the seemingly 'hard' decisions of businesses about whether to adopt new productive technologies are heavily influenced by the political environment in which they have to be made. How much power does organised labour have to challenge and disrupt decisions that will affect their membership? In the extreme case—reached in 1985/86 at Wapping—how far will the Home Office sanction police protection for those who make a quantum leap in technology and thereby disrupt conventional labour relations in industry? ... And that is merely a way of asking how opinion leaders in society at large view the redistribution of wealth and power associated with a particular technological change. We are back yet again with values and power.

### 3. THE UNDERSIDE OF TECHNOLOGICAL CHOICE

It may be helpful at this point to summarise the main thrust of this whole section. I have looked at three areas of rapid technical change—nuclear power, biotechnologies, and robotics and automation. There are some who would argue that these technologies are unstoppable. They have their own momentum which cannot be controlled. Others would argue that these technologies do indeed have their own momentum, but that momentum derives from the fact that they are developed from and set within the social and economic environment of competitive capitalism. It is the constant search for competitive superiority that makes technology uncontrollable. I wish to resist neither of these arguments, but I cannot accept them as the whole truth. I believe them to be important but partial perceptions whose partiality is in fact extremely dangerous. If we once convince ourselves that technology is uncontrollable, then questions about its control and, more particularly, about its social appropriateness and the distribution of its costs and benefits become redundant. If the whole technological enterprise is determined by scientific or economic forces, then the entire area of discourse is closed to us.

It is for this reason that it seems so important to put questions of values and power—which are almost identical to questions of justice—back in their rightful place at the heart of discussions about technology. There are, of course, powerful drives that come from the nature of science itself and from the profit motive: but those powerful drives can be modified, redirected, diverted, perhaps even impeded by deliberate acts of social choice. We can turn our back on nuclear power. We can turn our back on organ transplants. We can turn our back on biotechnologies that multiply the use of herbicides. But we can do so only when we have faced two sets of questions: 'What are going to be the long-term consequences of accepting and rejecting these technologies? And how are the costs and benefits associated with these technologies going to be distributed?' Once we can answer those questions we can then put technical decisions where they belong—in the domain of public discussion and, ultimately, political decision.

That, however, raises some further questions to which we must finally turn.

## 4. BUT WHAT CAN I DO?

As with most of the issues with which we have been concerned in this book, an appropriate reaction to the issues that we have introduced is a feeling of despair and powerlessness. Once we abandon the naive optimism of Modrzhinskaya and Buckminster Fuller, and accept that technology both creates and reflects the wider society in which it is set, we inevitably feel caught up in processes in which no one person or organisation has control, and indeed in which few of us even have influence. Yet as we began to see in the last section, the acceptance of a supine impotence, whether borne of despair, carelessness or callousness, is in fact going to make the nightmare of determinism a reality.

So how can we be responsible? If Bertrand de Juvenal is right that 'our membership of a technologically advanced society is ... a privilege', by what means can we accept responsibility for that privilege?

I want to suggest three areas in which I think the answers to those questions lie.

The first was put by Jacques Ellul himself like this:

> Men must be convinced that technical progress is not humanity's supreme adventure ... as long as man worships technique, there is as good as no chance that he will ever succeed in mastering it.

Our society is in danger of making technology an idolatry. That is, of ascribing to technology a value, a worth, a place in society that is beyond challenge. Technology thus becomes the yardstick by which other features and virtues are measured. Technical efficiency takes primacy over aesthetics. Technique takes primacy over the humanity of what technique accomplishes. In its most extreme form, technique becomes not a means but an end in itself. That is precisely what happened to the American space programme in its heyday.

The first step in dethroning technology, to chasing it back to its proper place in the order of things, is not to belittle it or detract from its intellectual fascination or its power to set men and women free from drudgery, but, rather, to erect around it and over it other values and wisdoms that oblige us to see technology in its correct perspective. The great themes of the meaning of life, the redemptive potential of death and suffering, the astonishing insights of artistic intuition, the recovery of a sense of the cosmic scale of the human tragedy and the human comedy, all that in earlier ages different cultures have understood by wisdom, and all that is supposed to be reflected in and meditated upon through religious consciousness—these are the powers that reduce an upstart lust for technique to its proper place.

This is not to plead for a dreary re-run of a dialogue of the deaf between 'science' and 'religion'. It is, rather, to encourage the rediscovery of cultural preoccupations that address issues far greater, though far more numinous, than can ever be addressed by technology. At the individual—and even congregational—level, that may involve some hard choices of how time and resources are spent. Are they spent on worshipping technique, whether it be in the crude forms of the video recorder or the microwave, or the more subtle forms of musical technique or liturgical perfection? Or are they committed, rather, to building up a cultural awareness, a creative consciousness of the great issues of life and death? Even in our churches, and much more in our homes and our popular art forms, we seem to have lost touch with the great questions that have fascinated, puzzled, irritated, and even driven mad the philosophers and artists of history. No wonder our culture becomes dominated by technology when, in Eliot's phrase, 'we lay waste our powers' in the search for the trivial, the instantaneous and the putrescent. If as individuals or communities or larger societies we abandon the search for meaning, for harmony, for eternity, or, to put it in religious

language, if we abandon the search for the kingdom of God, other preoccupations will claim our attention, our time, our creativity. And because it offers or seems to offer so much, so quickly and with such an appealing mystique, technology will be amongst the first of those preoccupations to fill the vacuum we have created.

The first step to taking responsibility for technology is therefore, paradoxically, to put it in its place. And the only way we can put it in its proper place is by putting other things in their proper place. And for Christians, those other things are neatly summarised by the phrase 'the kingdom of God'.

Although that is the prior, the fundamental task, it is of course not alone. By knocking technology off its perch we do not clip its wings. To do that, to keep it as servant rather than master, we have to learn to assess it. That very phrase causes some people surprise. 'Can technology be assessed?' they ask. 'Surely it either exists or it doesn't exist. It can no more be assessed than the moon or the wind.'

I hope I have raised sufficient questions about sufficient examples of technology in this chapter to show that every technology can have two fundamental sets of questions asked about it: will it work, and is it benign? I have unpacked both questions into many

What will it be? Back to nature? Or on to new technologies?

subsets of questions which, taken together, indicate the scale of enquiry implied by technology assessment.

Although in the United States the discipline of technology assessment is fairly well advanced—at least judged in terms of the volume of professional literature—there is always the danger that it becomes an esoteric dialogue between two sets of experts. In Britain the quasi-judicial nature of planning enquiries, their increasing complexity, length, cost and non-democratic process tends to narrow the field to the professional lobbyists.

The one area in which we all have to make some kind of assessment of technology is in medicine. Will I take the specialist's advice and have this operation? Will I take this drug? Will I have an abortion? Will I encourage yet more investigative surgery on my weak and elderly mother? Yet, paradoxically, it is at this point, when we or those close to us are at the receiving end of the technology, that we are least able, and even least fitted, to make any kind of realistic assessment of the technology concerned in its wider social setting.

That situation, however, does emphasise one central feature of technology assessment. If we have to make a decision about the application to our own bodies of a particular medical theory, we take good care to know the facts. Will it work? What are the costs? What are the benefits? What are the risks? What are the uncertainties? What are the alternatives? We take a good deal of trouble to put ourselves in a position where we can make a responsible choice in the light of the most complete and reliable assembly of facts that we can muster.

We are much less likely to look at the other side of the equation. For us, this is our health. That becomes an ultimate value for which we are prepared to sacrifice practically everything.

That is why as a patient we are not in a very good position to assess medical technology. We need certainly the patient's awareness of the facts: but we need too an emotional and psychological distance from the outcome of whatever decision is made about the application of specific technology. For example, the people making the series of decisions to carry on developing Concorde—an almost classic example of an inappropriate and wasteful technology—needed to look not just at whether the technology was economically and technically feasible, but at what benefits could have been achieved if the resources devoted to the development of Concorde had been put to other uses. As a patient, that is not a question I can be expected to ask very insistently: as a member of a society that is trying to take responsibility for its own technology it is a question I cannot avoid asking.

There is no more important question to be asked. For it forces us to look critically and creatively at what the real priorities for the future of technology are. If we pour money into the technology of destruction, the technologies of high tech toys and of high cost medicine, we are as a society proclaiming that a high capacity to kill, a high capacity to titillate the appetites of the rich and restore the bodies of the few, are the best uses to which human ingenuity can be put. I burlesque the argument to make the point. Every decision about the commitment of research and development resources is finally a statement about social priorities. To be responsible for the privilege of technology is precisely to confront that question with all the intellectual and moral energy that any question about the shaping of creation must command.

After we have knocked technology off its perch and clipped its wings by assessing its place in social priorities, there are two more tasks ahead of us. The first is to ensure that society is sufficiently 'open' to allow the discussions implied in the last few paragraphs to take place. The threat of technological authoritarianism has always been present, but is certainly growing. It is easy to see why. The costs and risks involved in the deployment of many new

Each branch of technology seems to have its own family of demons. As passengers are shuttled at supersonic speed over the Atlantic, the exhaust fumes of Concorde contribute to the erosion of the earth's protective ozone layer.

technologies, from nuclear power to satellite broadcasting, are very high indeed, and the potential damage that will result from making the wrong decision is proportionately grave. Under these circumstances, openness, even in the public domain, becomes increasingly hard to preserve. In the private domain, where technological progress is converted eventually into potentially enormous profits, secrecy becomes all. Writing of the privatisation of much scientific research, Kenny and Buttel have this to say:

> The ... most ominous implication is the growing prevalence of trade secrecy which will likely begin to erode the free flow of scientific information among scientists and from laboratories ...

Clearly, if a technology is developed in secret and only made public in the form of a product for sale, it is already too late to raise questions about the social value of research and development resources committed to the exploration of that technology. Those resources have already been spent. Equally, it is much more difficult to withstand the commercialisation of that technology once the product is on the market.

For obvious reasons, the tendency towards technological authoritarianism is greatest in the area of defence. For example, we do not know and are probably unlikely ever to know, what technologies now exist in the areas of germ warfare, gas warfare and warfare in space. There is no better antidote to public assessment of technology than total ignorance.

I have put a great deal of emphasis throughout this chapter on technology as the product and bearer of values, and technology as bestower and creature of power. In setting technology in a wider universe of discourse and in trying to assess its impact on society, we are already beginning to engage in the most fundamental task of all, namely the creation and protection of values that we see as central and the critical challenge of concentrations of power that subvert technology for their own purposes. I want to finish this chapter by saying a little bit more about both of these areas.

It is much easier to write about 'the creation of social values' than to do it. For most of us most of the time, such phrases seem stratospheric. Yet that can be an illusion. Social values are created in the pub, the chippy, the canteen, at the school gate and on the football terrace, as well as in Parliament, Synod, Broadcasting House and Fleet Street. Who leads whom in this area is never clear. We need only to ask ourselves where the sexual revolution of the sixties came from to see the ambiguity. That is not to say that the

A soldier in an anti-radioactivity suit trains for limited nuclear warfare.

ability to create a social climate is entirely evenly spread, or that a widow in Blackburn has the same social influence as an editor in Wapping. It is to insist that we make ourselves powerless when we maintain that we have no power. Clearly we can enlarge the scale of our influence by taking an intelligent, informed interest in every forum of public debate open to us—from our local PTA or union branch meeting, to the columns of the local press, the surgeries of local politicians and the councils of our church. Whatever one's views on abortion, at least on that issue there has been a degree of debate and conflict which has meant that many people have had to make up their own minds and decide where they stand.

But the example of abortion warns us of something else. The creation of social values is never conflict-free, and is always imperfect. The values that emerge, around which, that is, a politically actionable consensus begins to form, will usually fall far short of what we may envision of the kingdom of God. As Niebhur reminds us, society is always immoral. That should move us neither to despair nor to anger, but rather to prophecy. It is when the Church lives out its vocation to be a prophetic community constantly challenging society to approach a little closer to the values of the kingdom that it discovers its true identity. And living in that tension between the values of the kingdom and the values of society we shall need all the graces of tolerance, humour, perseverance and faith that a living spirituality can put us in touch with.

For we shall constantly see power abused and misused, and we shall constantly be aware of the way in which that power itself abuses the technical creativity that is our special privilege. We are, as it were, called into permanent opposition, into permanent challenge and criticism of a society that will always seem incapable of living redemptively with its own technical brilliance. We do not have to be led by the nose by technology: but while we live in a human society that has not awoken to the reality of its redemption, we need not expect to lead technology by the nose either. We are neither bound nor free. That is both the tragedy and the comedy of the human situation.

## PRAYER

Prayer for this area is prayer that humankind might rediscover a wisdom that both controls technology and gives proper recognition to all the virtues that make people more fully human and thus potentially more divine.

We have discovered that the central categories are values and power, and it would therefore be good to start into the prayer by going back to the Bible readings from that perspective. What do those readings tell us about the values that technology should reflect? (You will probably find Exodus, Genesis, and 1 Corinthians the three most fertile passages in this connection, but it may be helpful to touch on the others too.)

Why does our society find those values so hard? Perhaps a good way into that question is to ask ourselves why *we* find them so hard. What is it deep in each of us that makes it so difficult to live the freedom that Christ died to give us? Why are we constantly tempted to make technology into a false god? Why do we care so little about the distribution of the benefits when we assume they accrue to us: and so much when they accrue to someone else?

Again, it is important to stress that the purpose of this style of praying is not to afflict us with guilt: it is rather to help us to see that we cannot take collective responsibility for the development of technology until we take responsibility, both individual and collective, for the maintenance of value systems that shape that technology. A return to the passage from St John might be a good idea at this point: where and how is the prince of darkness being overthrown? And how do we live that out?

We might then move on to think about questions of power. It is always easy to see the power that others enjoy—and abuse at our expense. It is less easy sometimes to see the power that we have as individuals and collectives. It is still harder to see that power under the judgment of God. You might find an imaginative reconstruction of Jerusalem at the time of Jeremiah helpful in this connection. Where was power in that society—and what did Yahweh do with it?

If then we can start our prayer by allowing God to help us see the links between our own inner drives and the social environment which our technology reflects, we can begin to pray without hypocrisy for the transformation of the world which St John sees Jesus having accomplished. That transformation is no less for humanity's ingenuity and creativity than it is for the Church or the natural environment or the poorest of the poor. All stand in need of redemption—and all are offered redemption. We pray for that offer to be taken up.

But that prayer has to be earthed, to be made as concrete as possible. Yes, we long for the redemption of the whole cosmos, and if we are mystically gifted, we might be able to pray that in a sustained and disciplined way. Most of us need something more tangible, more hard-edged to give life and sharpness to our prayers. So ask yourself where you are becoming aware of technology standing in need of redemption. It may be in one of the areas we have explored; or it may be something quite different, something you have observed in your own community, even in your own family. That is a good place to start ...

For that is the kairos for you, now. It is the moment of opportunity for you to confront the powers that would subvert a gift of God and make it a power that destroys and enslaves. It may do so in very direct and obvious ways, like amniocentesis to abort female foetuses. Or it may be much more insidious: the privatisation of genetic material to bestow huge power on a few corporations (with the corollary of a few individuals within those corporations). The kairos consists precisely of this: that as we become aware of these abuses of one of God's greatest gifts, we have the opportunity to be co-opted by their perpetrators. Or to resist.

I believe there is no more powerful resistance than a spirituality that binds together the five elements of reflection, analysis, prayer, action and appraisal.

## ACTION

Let me admit at once that of the five areas we look at in this book, this one is the most difficult for which to produce an instant 'action pack'. That is partly because the subject itself is more subterranean than the others; partly because non-experts feel instantly disabled by the technical jargon of the experts; and partly because pressure groups, recognising both these handicaps, tend to cluster round the outward symptoms, such as pollution or compensation for the victims of iatrogeneric diseases, rather than the fundamental causes. Yet in confronting technological determinism and the technical irresponsibility of governments and corporations, there is no field in which informed Christian action is more appropriate.

### BUT HOW TO START?

It is unlikely that we can master the intricacies of the technology of any one discipline, never mind a whole battery of disciplines. We can, though, inform ourselves of where the real questions are in any one discipline, whether it be nuclear power, genetic engineering, particular branches of medicine, communications, or whatever. There is a growing literature, some of it quoted above, that seeks to bring the lay person up to date with the ethical questions posed by the technologies concerned. Further, some Church denominations have published reports in this area—and often been disappointed by the seeming lack of response from their church members to the issues they have tried to raise. One excellent example is *Future Conditional: Science, Technology and Society—a critical Christian View* published in 1983 by the Home Division of the Methodist Church. It can usefully be seen as a comment on the well-known study by the World Council of Churches, published in 1980 as *Faith and Science in an Unjust World*.

If there is no easy alternative to reading oneself into a subject to learn the grammar, there are groups on hand who can help take one further after even quite modest reading. Two such are the British Society for Social Responsibility in Science, and the Centre for Alternative Industrial and Technological Systems. While neither of these organisations is overtly Christian, they are able to help individuals and groups learn more about the issues and they can point to specific problems on which political or social action is urgently needed.

Another useful source of helpful expertise may turn out to be the local university or polytechnic. For many practising scientists are themselves deeply bothered by the failure of society as a whole to engage in fundamental debate about where technology is leading us and where the real priorities lie. Christian scientists—of whom there are many more than one might expect—often feel marginalised and ignored by the churches and to that extent welcome an opportunity to think aloud about these problems. (They can usually be located with the help of the university or polytechnic chaplains.)

Let's suppose that a small group of people has done its homework on a particular issue: say the balance between high tech medicine and preventative medicine in the NHS; or the implications of the widespread adoption of computer assisted design and manufacturing in British industry (CADCAM). What then?

In this area, it is unlikely that there is one single decision that will reverse the trend; it is unlikely too that there will be one single body (either individual or corporate) who can take that decision. We are back with the subterranean nature of the subject. So what can we do? What action can we take that discharges our obligation of responsibility?

One approach is what the Americans call Citizen Awareness, and what we might be more comfortable calling public debate. We have to find strategies for getting the issue discussed—not only by the experts and the powerful but by Mr and Mrs Joe Average. They have the right to know what is going on and they have the right to make their contribution to the debate. Including them in that debate is going to be a hard struggle because the expert and the professional would far rather leave them out, as we have seen in so many planning enquiries and so-called exercises in public consultation.

Techniques for informing and engaging them will vary from badgering local radio and television companies to air the subject and follow it up with a phone-in; to using existing networks within and outside the Church, like the Mothers' Union (much derided in some circles, but a group of people with greater intelligence and clout than they are usually given credit for by the trendies), the Women's Institute (ditto), trade unions and Trades Councils, Rotary and its parallels, Chambers of Commerce, Parent Teacher Associations and political parties. The object, remember, is not to sell a particular line (though it is probable that your group will develop a line as it gets into the subject) but rather to inform people and to encourage them to come to their own conclusions. Perhaps one of the harder parts of this exercise is to listen patiently and open-mindedly to those conclusions. Some will be astonishingly wise; others plain daft. All have the right to be heard and the right of access to further information to go on crystallising their thinking.

As this process develops, it is likely that a consensus will emerge that calls for change in existing practice or policy. Such demands may be directed towards a range of actors—from government departments, to multinational firms to, let us say, a local council or Health Authority. It may be something huge, like the abandonment of the nuclear power programme; or it may be relatively minor like an increase in the proportion of funds devoted to preventative medicine. Either way, the ground rules sketched in earlier chapters still apply: be well-informed; build as many alliances as possible to maximise support in the community; be firm but patient; remember the power of even the local newspapers. And incorporate what you are doing in your own prayer life and in the liturgy of your worshipping community.

I have put a great deal of emphasis throughout this chapter on technology as the product and bearer of values: and as the bestower and creator of power. In setting its control in the wider social context I have assumed in the last few paragraphs, we are already beginning to engage in the most fundamental task of all: namely the creation and protection of values that we see as central. For it is that which will mount a critical challenge to the concentrations of power that subvert technology for their own purposes. But how do we create and protect those values?

On that the biblical record seems quite clear. It is by taking the low road. By giving up our security in favour of those who are insecure; by divesting ourselves of power in favour of those who are excluded from power; by refusing to be seduced by a technology that we do not need for the sake of those who are denied technologies that they require for survival ... this is the low road that St Matthew tells us in chapter 25 of his Gospel will show us the face of Christ himself. On the low road we shall find that God's voice and presence have been squeezed out of those places where the values of modern technology hold unchallenged sway. As the great American biblical scholar and prophet Walter Brueggemann has put it:

> The church is mandated not just to do kind things, but mandated to perceive the world differently; to know that the wave of the future is not in putting people down, but in raising them up; the fruit of the kingdom is not in excluding but in including. In this action and this teaching Jesus draws a sharp distinction between himself and the world's salvation systems, that is, the legal systems of competence and achievement (and, we may add, of technological superiority) ... No wonder Jesus was such a threat, because he placed into question the world's way of ordering its life, doing its business, rewarding its adherents and punishing its dissenters! ...

On the low road we certainly perceive the world differently. And it is in that perception and its sharing with others whose perspectives, we may well find, are complementary to our own, that we begin to create and protect the values of a society that is at least turning towards the kingdom.

That, however, is grace. It is gift. It is the power of the love of God, meeting us on the low road to convert us through repentance, through the gift of the power of the Spirit. And that is kairos.

## APPRAISAL

This is likely to be an awkward part of the cycle because of the very nature of the subject. Unlike some of the other issues we have been dealing with, this area is more fundamental but more abstract.

How then to appraise the cycle we have been following?

As in the other chapters, the first thing is to look at the integration of reflection, prayer and action. Because of the seemingly secular nature of the subject and the relative poverty of the Church's thinking in this area, it is unusually hard to hold the nuts and bolts of the debate in the right tension with private and public prayer. What precisely do we pray about? How exactly do we bring the biblical material, coming as it does from a pre-technical milieu, to bear on the highly technical issues we find ourselves engaged in?

There are, of course, no simple answers to those questions. All I can do here is to encourage you to go on wrestling with them, confident that you are in the right place if you are trying, however inadequately you may feel it to be, to proclaim the primacy of the values of the kingdom of God in the stuff of our technical society. To proclaim those values you will need to live them—and to live them you will need all the grace that an active prayer life can bring you.

Perhaps there is no other area where we are more likely to be afflicted with an overwhelming sense of hopelessness, despair and frustration. The issues are so big, so veiled in jargon and technicality that we feel that they are literally beyond us. There is nothing, we tell ourselves, that we can do.

However understandable and reasonable such feelings may be, whether at the individual or group level, they delight the Principalities and Powers of this present world because they anticipate our withdrawal from the field to leave it free for 'Them'. Once we surrender to our own fears and (no doubt proper) acknowledgements of our limitations in the technical grounding of the subject, as though that alone gave us the right to think, pray and act, we are well on the way to becoming part of the prevailing idolatry.

Gripped by such fears, a return to basics might help: our task is less to master the intricacies of technical detail than to call our civilisation to look at the wider questions that so easily get occluded by fascination with technique.

In our appraisal, then, it is important to hold that perspective in the centre of our reflection. What are we involved in that dethrones technique, that points to other, more healthful, 'supreme adventures'?

For that, I suspect, is where most of us will find our point of entry. We cannot become expert microbiologists or physicists overnight—or perhaps in a lifetime. But we can become, perhaps already are in embryo, creators of a counter-culture, a counter consciousness that refuses to allow technique to hijack the human spirit.

So there is a rich vein for your appraisal! Where have you or can you chase technique back to its own lair by living the values, the life, that say health and wholeness are of more value than technical sophistication? Maybe the only way we can subvert this unbound Prometheus is not by direct confrontation, but by constructing other realities to contain it. And that is a demanding task indeed, in which we shall ever live in conscious need of the companionship of the Spirit.

# CONCLUSION

It remains only to pull together the central themes of this book. We need to do that at three levels: the substantive, the prayerful, and the community. This pulling together is a necessary corrective rather than a postscripted afterthought. For the danger of the method I have adopted in this book is that by neatly dividing subjects and processes, I misrepresent what is really a whole, an organic entity whose integrity is fundamental to all that I have been writing about. A morbid anatomist can dissect tissue and examine ligaments and bones. That has a useful purpose in understanding what makes the human body work. But it says nothing about life. Yet I hope this book is ultimately about life rather than ligaments and bones.

It is perhaps easiest to see this at the level of the analysis that I have introduced. In many chapters I have had to create artificial barriers to enable the material to be handled, and even so, one subject has tended to seep into another. For example, you cannot discuss poverty without discussing the environment and technology. You cannot discuss technology without raising issues of power and community. You cannot discuss militarism without considering international politics and the effect of militarisation on the poor of the world, whether 'out there' or 'right here'. The kairos that is presented to us in one area of our life inevitably calls us into a creative and trustful response in other areas. Because God made a world that reflects his wholeness, we cannot compartmentalise it into bite-sized chunks that reflect only the size of our appetites.

That presents us with a serious problem. The world and its kairos are so marvellously knit together and interravelled, that to disaggregate it, break it down and chop it up is to do violence to a central fact about the glory of God. How can we honour that fact, the wholeness of God, in our response to the kairos of our times, when we are constantly brought up against the limitations of energy, time, information, resources and enthusiasm? How, to adopt the analogy of the first paragraph, can we be sure that we are dealing with life rather than inspecting bones—without running ourselves into the ground so that we can neither reflect, pray nor analyse creatively?

It seems to me that the answer to that question lies in holding together two perspectives that seem, superficially at least, to be mutually exclusive. The first is the wisdom of 'blooming where you are planted'. That is to say, we are all in a given environment, with a given set of contacts, points of entry and possibilities. As we become aware of the kairos with which we are being faced, the temptation is to imagine that we would be able to respond to it much better by moving somewhere else, changing our job, changing our skills, changing our religion. Without wishing to rule out the possibility that we will indeed be called to make some such radical change in our lives, the first assumption has to be that God invites us into a response where we are and as we are. Of course, the very fact of a response will change us, perhaps profoundly, but that change will begin in the 'inner' dimension. And it is as well to let that be worked out properly before we embark on the major changes of our lives to which it may in time lead.

The response will almost certainly start here, with this dozy parish, this complacent MP, this purblind Council, this demoralised group of ex-activists. And it will start, too, with this untrusting, frightened, angry and uncentred soul which in some way that we only dimly perceive at present is in solidarity with the sin of the world—and is called into the glory of God's redemption of it.

The first side of the paradox, then, is that we must start with what we have and where we are, accepting all the limitations and weakness that that implies. But the second side is to enter imaginatively and prayerfully into the wholeness of God as reflected in the wholeness of his creation. We might not be able to *do* anything today about the arms trade or even the pollution of our local river, but we can offer both to God as the outworkings of a human condition that desperately needs delivering from itself.

Then what we *do* do, in prayer and action, assumes a representative quality. It not only has its own validity and integrity, we hope, but also it stands for something much bigger and more encompassing. Maybe all I can do is to join Greenpeace and get my parish to reflect the kairos of the environment more regularly in its worship and teaching. That may feel so small and inadequate a response that I am tempted to give up because, 'It won't make any difference.' But in doing what I am doing and allowing myself to be changed in the process, I am plugging into the power of God at work in his world. My weakness and his power can be a surprisingly potent mixture—in ways that go far beyond the immediate concerns of my outward activity. And the more I can reflect on what I am doing in prayer, meditation and contemplation, the more potent that mixture can become.

I want to get the nuance right, because the dangers of being misunderstood at this point are great. I am not saying: 'In the end it doesn't greatly matter how little or how much you do: remember to pray for the world and all will be well.' Nor am I encouraging a retreat into the trivial or the parochial. Rather I am trying to warn against three sets of dangers that I constantly encounter in myself and the people who give me the privilege of working with them. The first is burn-out, as a result of taking on too much, too quickly, with inadequate spiritual foundations. The second is guilt at being unable to achieve all that needs to be achieved. And the third is despair because what has been accomplished seems so small and insignificant on the scale of human misery and structural sinfulness. If we learn to bloom where we are planted and yet honour the greatness and unity of God and his creation, we may be able to find a way round these three dangers.

For they all stem, at bottom, precisely from a correct insight into the interpenetration of the subjects of the foregoing chapters. '*All* have fallen short of the glory of God ...', and we somehow feel that each of us will reflect that glory less inadequately only as we all reflect it. That is the inner meaning of a cliché that has begun to wear thin. 'Interdependence' is certainly a social and political reality that our culture has ignored too long: but its most important and most neglected reality can only be understood in a metaphysical sense. We need a spirituality that simultaneously puts us in touch with the oneness of creation—and liberates and encourages us to do what we can, where we can, with the resources we have, to work with God's redeeming love for that creation.

After I had written the paragraphs above, I had to go to a meeting in London. As I sat on the tube, I was wondering whether I had said what I wanted to say and whether I had said it right. In one of those luminous moments of synchronicity, my eye was drawn to a woman sitting opposite me. She was middle-aged, brown, lumpy, with a strong West Indian accent that suggested that she may not have been long in this country. There was nothing remarkable about her. But she was wearing an anorak, above the breast pocket of which were embroidered four words that said precisely what I have been trying to say. They read: 'We are the world.' Quite.

It is holding together that perception with the loving majesty of

God that challenges the wholeness or integrity of our prayer. As I have explained the cycle of reflection, analysis, prayer, action and appraisal, there is a danger, not only that the prayer may somehow get delinked from the other components, but also that it may lose breadth and depth just because it is set in the cycle that I have proposed. At the bottom of that lies the danger that, paradoxically, we make gods of our subjects of concern—the environment or militarism or technology—and thus lose the centre of what prayer is all about. Once we try to manipulate God into taking our side, doing what we want, reflecting our priorities and prejudices, we have ceased to pray to the God of the Old and New Testament and have begun to pray to a projection of ourselves. And that is at once the most subtle and most disastrous form of idolatry.

It is easier to recognise the general danger than to be precise about how to avoid it. For it can take many forms and the prince of darkness lacks no ingenuity in inventing new ones. I personally find that a conscious attempt to give back to God whatever it is that I am praying about is a healthy corrective to the semi-conscious conviction that I am in charge and God would be well advised to do what I suggest. My most striking reminder of the need of that came when I was contemplating leaving Christian Aid. In prayer, I was

What hope is there for the future of humankind? Can the deep divisions that separate people from people ever be healed?

conscious of being invited to get off an overcrowded and long-delayed tube train. I protested. After all I was on my way, late already, to an important meeting, one in which crucial decisions affecting thousands of poor people would be made. 'They're your poor, Lord,' I said, insinuating that he should take care of them by kindly not interrupting my journey.

'Quite,' he answered. 'They are mine. And not yours ...'

The final level at which I want to appeal for wholeness is what I called the community level above. I have expressed most of this book in terms of the personal, the individual, with only occasional references to the group or community—whether church-based or entirely secular—in which much of the analysis and action will properly be set. What I want to emphasise here is the fact that just as the individual is located in some kind of group, so each group is located in a larger social network. It can be important to hang on to that. As we struggle to engage in action via the Lower Piddlecombe Naturalists Group, we may find ourselves wondering just what we can achieve. It then becomes helpful to realise that the Lower Piddlecombians are not alone. There is a whole array of analogous organisations, some more alive than others, but all trying to play their part in the process.

This, then, is a plea for a wider look at the total setting in which our prayer and action are set. However alone we may feel at times, the truth is that we are not alone—either in the trivial sense of the last paragraph, nor in the much profounder sense that our prayer is, if it has its own integrity, caught up in the prayer of Christ himself. If we can begin to apprehend the wholeness of the community of which we are members, the community, that is, that includes the living and the dead, past, present and future generations with Christ at its head, then we need never be overly depressed by the smallness of our outreach or the weakness of the group with which we work and pray.

The three points I have made in this conclusion—the interdependence of all things in the unity of all creation; the centredness of prayer on the person of Christ; and the communion of all the saints—all underline the final plea of this book. The fact that you have read it thus far (or at all) suggests that you are one who is disposed to take the world seriously. You want to be alive to the kairos I have tried to describe and to do your part to enable men and women to make the kind of response that will bring salvation to the world. You are not afraid of the consequences of that decision, because most of the time you are able to trust the Lord on whose love you have been reflecting.

Now learn to be gentle with yourself. That is not, of course, an invitation to complacency or pietism or a callous withdrawal. It is rather a reflection of God's love and care for you and your community. Let me put it in the words of an older, deeper wisdom:

> The novice was so rigorous in all the disciplines of the godly life that he hardly slept; ate next to nothing; went barefoot on the bitterest night and never had a word of complaint or a harsh thing to say of any of his brothers. The Lord rewarded him with a dream in which he was present at the scourging of the Saviour. The novice was full of terror and pity for the wounds that the whips were making. 'Let me take your place,' he cried, rushing to the whipping post and covering the Saviour's back with his own.
>
> 'No, no,' said the Saviour. 'That is not right.'
>
> 'Then at least let me be beaten too, so that I may share your suffering,' begged the novice.
>
> At that the Saviour became sad and severe. 'If you do that,' he said, 'you do not understand my calling. It is to save you that I am here; not to subject you to the same sufferings. I must endure ... Move to one side, please; let the soldiers continue.'
>
> When he awoke, the novice had a good meal and put shoes on his feet. And the brothers said he would soon be ready to be a full member of their brotherhood.

# Organisations

**PEACE**
Campaign for Nuclear Disarmament.
Christian CND.
Christian Movement for Peace.
Christian Peace Conference.
Council on Christian Approaches to
 Defence & Disarmament.
Dept of Peace Studies,
 University of Bradford.
Evangelical Peacemakers.
Fellowship of Reconciliation.
National Peace Council.
Pax Christi.
Peace Pledge Union.
Peace Tax Campaign.
War Resisters International.
Women's International League for
 Peace and Freedom.
World Disarmament Campaign.

**POVERTY**
Action Aid.
Christian Aid.
Oxfam.
Traidcraft.
Tear Fund.
World Development Movement.
The following Universities have departments or institutes that specialise in third world issues: Sussex, Swansea, East Anglia, Oxford, Manchester and Birmingham.

**ENVIRONMENT**
Friends of the Earth.
Greenpeace.
Green Deserts.
Council for the Preservation of
 Rural England/Wales.
World Resources Institute,
 1735 New York Avenue NW,
 Washington DC 20006, USA
 —the NGO spearheading the
 Tropical Forestry Action Plan.

**COMMUNITY**
Alliance of Radical Methodists.
Baptist Renewal Group.
Christian Socialist Movement.
Christians against Racism and
 Fascism.
Joint Council for the Welfare of
 Immigrants.
Urban Ministry Project.

**TECHNOLOGY**
British Society for Social
 Responsibility in Science.
Centre for Alternative Industrial
 and Technological Systems.
Centre for Alternative Technology.
Intermediate Technology
 Development Group.
Schumacher Centre.
Science or Society?

# Further Reading

The following are grouped according to chapter. The books are arranged roughly in accordance with the knowledge of the subject they assume. The first book(s) are therefore a less demanding read than the last. None is so technical as to be impenetrable to all but the academic expert.

**INTRODUCTION**

Jim Wallis, *Agenda for Biblical People*, SPCK (1986).
J.R.W. Stott, *Issues Facing Christians To-day*, Marshall Pickering (1984).
Lesslie Newbigin, *Foolishness to the Greeks: The Gospel and Western Culture*, SPCK (1986).
Paul Oestreicher, *The Double Cross: Christianity in a world that's dying to Live*, DLT (1986).
Haddon Willmer (ed), *Christian Faith and Political Hopes*, Epworth (1979).
Walter Wink, *Naming the Powers* and *Unmasking the Powers*, Fortress (1984 and 1986 respectively).

**CHAPTER 1**

CAFOD, *Africa's Crisis and the Church in Britain*, CTS (1987).
Independent Group on British Aid, *Missed Opportunities: Britain and the Third World*, IGBA (1986).
Frances Moore Lappe and Joseph Collins, *World Hunger: Twelve Myths*, Grove (1986).
Charles Elliott, *Comfortable Compassion? Poverty, Power and the Church*, Hodder (1987).
R. Jolly and A. Cornia, *The Impact of World Recession on Children*, Pergamon (1984).
R. Jolly, F. Stewart and A. Cornia, *Adjustment with a Human Face*, Oxford (1987).
Jacobo Schatan, *World Debt: Who is to Pay?* Zed (1987).

**CHAPTER 2**

Gro Harlem Brundtland (chair), *Our Common Future: The World Commission on Environment and Development*, Oxford (1987).
Food and Agriculture Organization, *The Tropical Forestry Action Plan*, FAO (Rome, 1987)
Eric Eckholm, *Down to Earth*, Norton (1981).
K. Ruddle and W. Manshard, *Renewable Natural Resources and the Environment:*

Pressing Problems in the Developing World, Tycooly (Dublin, 1982).
The Tropical Agriculture Association (UK), *Tropical Agriculturists: Future Prospects*, British Council (1987).

**CHAPTER 3**

P.J. O'Mahony, *Multinationals and Human Rights*, Mayhew McCrimmon (1980).
Austin Smith, *Passion for the Inner City*, Sheed & Ward (1983).
Colin Brewer, Terence Morris, Patricia Morgan, Maurice North, *Criminal Welfare on Trial*, Social Affairs Unit (1981).
S. Kumar (ed), *The Schumacher Lectures*, Blond & Briggs (1980).
A.S. Cigler (ed), *Interest Group Politics*, C.Q. Press (1986).
Niels Bjorn Anderson, *The Information Society: For Richer, For Poorer...*, North Holland (1982).
Graham Wilson, *Interest Groups in the United States*, Oxford (1984).

**CHAPTER 4**

E.P. Thompson, *Protest and Survive*, CND/Bertrand Russell Peace Foundation (1980).
Mary Kaldor, *The Baroque Arsenal*, Deutsch (1982).
Independent Commission on Disarmament and Security Issues (chair: Olof Palme), *Common Security: A Programme for Disarmament*, Pan (1982).
*Disarmament and World Development: Is there a way forward?* Institute of Development Studies *IDS Bulletin* 16:4 (October 1985).
Swedish International Peace Research Institute, *Yearbook*.
Robin Luckham, 'Armament Culture' in *Alternatives* (Summer 1984).

**CHAPTER 5**

Home Mission Division of the Methodist Church, *Future Conditional: Science, Technology and Society—a critical Christian view* (1983).
Amory B. Lovins, *Soft Energy Paths: Toward a Durable Peace*, Harper (1980).
Edward Yoxen, *The Genes Business: who should control biotechnology?*, Pan (1983).
Mike Hales, *Science or Society: The politics of the work of scientists*, Free Association Books (1986).
Ralph Kaplinsky, *Automation: the technology and society*, Longman (1984).
L. Doyal, *The political economy of health*, Pluto (1979).
N. Elias and eds, 'Scientific Establishments and Hierarchies' in *Sociology of the Sciences Yearbook 6*, Elsevier (1982).
S. Krimsky, *Genetic Alchemy: a social history of the recombinant DNA controversy*, MIT Press (1982).

# INDEX

## Bible passages